Contents

If ... Then ... Curriculum: Assessment-Based Instruction, Grade 2

Lucy Calkins with Julia Mooney and Colleagues from the Teachers College Reading and Writing Project

Photography by Peter Cunningham

HEINEMANN ◆ PORTSMOUTH, NH

*first*hand
An imprint of Heinemann
361 Hanover Street
Portsmouth, NH 03801–3912
www.heinemann.com

Offices and agents throughout the world

Cataloging-in-Publication data is on file with the Library of Congress.

ISBN-13: 978-0-325-04812-3
ISBN-10: 0-325-04812-6

Production: Elizabeth Valway, David Stirling, and Abigail Heim
Cover and interior designs: Jenny Jensen Greenleaf
Series includes photographs by Peter Cunningham, Nadine Baldasare, and Elizabeth Dunford
Composition: Publishers' Design and Production Services, Inc.
Manufacturing: Steve Bernier

Printed in the United States of America on acid-free paper
17 16 15 14 13 VP 1 2 3 4 5

Introduction

Twenty-five years ago, in the first edition of the now classic *The Art of Teaching Writing*, I wrote a chapter on second-grade writers in which I argued that second-graders are not unlike adolescents. Like adolescents, second-graders experience a growth spurt that provides them with new power and ambition and sometimes leaves them a bit awkward. Like adolescents, some second-graders' bodies become all leggy, as if their newfound height has yet to be integrated and synthesized; so, too, their writing can be leggy. A coherent story has an ending that goes on and on and on; a report includes, in one chapter, a list containing thirteen items. It sometimes seems as if second-graders can write longer and faster and more than they can synthesize and control and structure. Some second-graders, then, will produce "the longest stories ever." Some will write reports and persuasive letters and speeches that are marked by a breathless quality, almost as if the entire draft is one gigantic run-on sentence.

Other second-graders are almost exactly the opposite—perhaps for related reasons. These second-graders write tight, conventional, brief drafts. "Is this right?" the youngster asks, repeatedly. The newfound concern with conventions and with "the right way to do things" relates to the new powers of this age. One of those newfound powers is the power to realize there is a right and a wrong way to do things and to worry about other people's judgments. Second-graders sometimes are marked with a new self-consciousness—and this can fuel tremendous learning, or it can do quite the opposite. This is an age when children who haven't learned cursive invent their own curlicue font in an effort to appear grown-up. Youngsters who aren't sure how to revise but know the teacher values revision will scissor apart a draft only to piece it back together again the exact same way, this time held together with tape. These youngsters will notice the conventions of a research report—the appendix, the captions, the charts and graphs—and want to emulate all of those things.

They will use exclamations and quotations and colons and parentheses with earnest resolve.

In this series, our treatment of second grade is not unlike our treatment of fifth grade. We handle both grade levels as if youngsters enter the school year with burgeoning powers, chomping at the bit to do something a bit new and very "cool." Second grade, like fifth grade, allows writers to extend the basic skills they will have developed during the previous two years writing workshops. In narrative writing, children are invited to study authors who not only record the true stories of what happened but who try to write those true stories as well as possible. In information writing, second-graders are challenged to extend their basic information writing skills to a new format— lab reports—and then are taught to write information books that draw on the traditional structure and language of science writing. In opinion writing, second-graders are invited to transfer their abilities to write about ideas and to support their ideas with evidence to their work in a unit on writing about reading. And to top this off, second-graders are invited to immerse themselves in a poetry writing workshop.

The four second-grade Units of Study books, then, do not tend to teach the basics of narrative, information, and opinion writing—the meat-and-potatoes curriculum—so much as they help students extend that curriculum, taking their basic skills further. The second-grade units that have been detailed in Units of Study books are especially beautiful, exciting, and relevant, but they are not especially foundational. And that is where this book comes in.

If your second-graders come to you without any prior experience in a writing workshop, this book will help you examine results from your on-demand writing assessments to ascertain whether your children will especially prosper if you teach a precursor unit prior to the units detailed in this series. That is, it is possible that you may find that students who do not have any prior background in the foundations of a writing workshop or of narrative, information, and opinion writing will respond best if you provide them with a foundation *before* they enter into some of these Units of Study books, and this book will help you make that decision. It will also help you provide that instruction if you determine it's what your students need.

On the opposite end of the spectrum, the book will also help you if your children came into this year with writing skills that are already progressing well, if they fly through the first four units and then are chomping at the bit for more. We recommend that a unit last no more than six weeks, so you'll have lots of time for additional units of study. This book suggests several alternative pathways you can take.

EXAMINE YOUR STUDENTS' INITIAL ON-DEMAND WRITING AND CHART A COURSE

If a large percentage of your students enter second grade unable to take up a several-page booklet and draw and write what happened one time when they did something, then you may decide it is necessary to teach a basic narrative writing unit before launching into *Lessons from the Masters*. This may not be the case, though. The *Lessons from the Masters* unit can be done in a very basic way. However, if you teach *Lessons from the Masters* to students who don't enter the workshop able to produce at least a bare-bones account of what they did one time, then you wouldn't be tapping into the potential of that unit for lifting students' narrative writing from good to great. What unit will best serve your students? These are the kinds of decisions you will need to make.

If you do decide to teach a basic narrative unit, I recommend any of three possible pathways. First, if you or your school own copies of the first edition of Units of Study for Primary Writing, you could use the *Small Moments* book from that series as the mainstay of your unit. We kept very little of that book in the new edition of *Small Moments*, so second-graders who have already been taught the new curriculum in first grade won't feel that book is a repeat. And although we've improved on that book mightily, it was always a favorite from the initial Units of Study series.

If this is the first year that your school is using the Units of Study series, a second option is for you to borrow the new *Small Moments* book from a first-grade colleague and to teach that unit to your second-graders. Then teach *Lessons from the Masters*. The challenge is that *Small Moments* will also be the first unit in your colleague's year, so you'd need to synchronize this with that

colleague. Your second-graders will never be first-graders again, so the fact that they are starting second-grade with a brand new, state-of-the-art, first-grade unit doesn't have many downsides, especially if they don't know this. (Make a book jacket!) The third solution is for you to rely on the first unit in this *If . . . Then . . .* book, "Launching with Small Moments," a new version of this popular unit especially angled toward second-graders.

One final point: your students may be able to write true stories of something they did, telling what happened bit by bit (their on-demand work may show their knowledge of narrative writing tends to at least fall within the developing category), but their spelling may be such that neither you nor the children can read their writing. If that's the case, you will want to immediately begin explicit instruction in phonics. By December of kindergarten, a teacher should be able to read most of what her children have written, and the children themselves should be able to read this as well (not that it will be conventional, but most of the sounds should be represented by letters). If your children have severe spelling problems, you will want to borrow the *Writing for Readers* unit from kindergarten, in addition to accelerating phonics instruction. We do not detail a phonics-heavy unit in this book, because it will be extremely rare for second-graders to be in such urgent need of phonics.

You may decide to do an on-demand assessment of information writing as well as of narrative writing at the very start of the year or you may decide to wait until just prior to teaching *Lab Reports and Science Books*. Either way, if your study of results shows that most of your children are not at the developing level in their abilities to write all-about texts, you have four choices you could make, and three of them match the choices you had for narrative writing. Again, if you have access to the initial Units of Study for Primary Writing series, you might decide to teach Part II of *Nonfiction Writing: Procedures and Reports* (Part I focuses on how-to writing). Another choice, once again, would be to borrow the first-grade book *Nonfiction Chapter Books* and teach that unit as a precursor to *Lab Reports and Science Books*. Finally, the alternative unit, "Information Books: Using Writing to Teach Others All about Our Favorite Topics," in this book will introduce your students to all-about books, helping them use nonfiction texts as mentors. It is aligned with the Common Core State Standards for second grade. For example, the standards expect second-graders to know how to ask and answer who, what, where, when, why, and how questions to understand key details in a text. Writers learn to do this sort of thing in this unit and will receive added practice in the *Lab Reports and Science Books* unit of study volume. Finally, you could bypass all of this, teach the first book in this series—*Lessons from the Masters*—and if your students flourish during the unit and if you end the unit with at least half your class approaching proficiency as narrative writers, you'll probably find they'll be able to use those skills in *Lab Reports and Science Books*.

By this time, your students will be able to handle *Writing about Reading*, which does not rely on a strong background in opinion writing, as well as *Poetry: Big Thoughts in Small Packages*. Neither of those units relies on students' having foundational knowledge of a particular genre.

Meanwhile, you may have taught all the units in this current Units of Study series and then want to extend your students' skills. The "Writing Gripping Fictional Stories with Meaning and Significance" unit in this book introduces students to realistic fiction and extends the work of *Lessons from the Masters* and also of the first-grade *Small Moments* volume. (It could just as easily be taught to third-graders as to second-graders.) It will help children write simple, realistic fiction stories, especially developing the plotline of those stories so the main character encounters trouble and then experiences rising tension before the story comes to a resolution—hence the title.

The "Persuasive Reviews" unit introduces students to the tools of persuasive writing and helps them write reviews with abandon, producing lots of informative, well-structured reviews of movies, restaurants, stores, video games, and the like. A simpler version of this unit is included in the first-grade series, so it's very accessible, supporting your more novice writers while also giving your proficient writers experience with what we sometimes refer to as "baby essays." If your students are not producing on-demand opinion pieces that are at least proficient before you teach this unit, they will be up to standard by the end of the unit.

And finally, "Independent Writing Projects Across the Genres" allows your students to transfer and apply all they have learned throughout the year to a writing project of their choice, teaching them that writers are deliberate in their decision about the best genre and form for their writing. This unit will infuse new life into your writing workshop, invigorating your students with new energy as they end the school year and head into the summer months.

Launching with Small Moments

RATIONALE/INTRODUCTION

This unit is meant not just as a narrative unit but also as an introductory unit. It brings children into the writing workshop, as well as into narrative writing. Children are taught, "You are writers, like writers the world over." Children learn to see their own lives as important and interesting and as a source of stories that are worth getting down on the page and sharing with the world. As you anticipate this unit, you will want to imagine that your children will be writing more than a dozen booklets within what will probably be four weeks, each booklet being first three and then five pages long. Children may at first write only a few sentences on a page (and they may write across only three pages), but before long they will write approximately one paragraph per page, five pages in a booklet, producing close to that amount of writing during each day's writing workshop. If that goal seems pie-in-the-sky to you, try to play the believing game and push your children to write more and more still, because your expectations are one of the most important determining factors in your classroom. It may be the case, however, that your children take a few months to be able to write as I'm describing—and that's okay. You start where your students are when they enter your classroom. The important thing is not where you start, but where you finish.

From the first day of the unit on, you will teach children to record the Small Moment stories of their lives. They'll write each of these in a booklet and they'll write lots of these, saving them in work-in-progress folders. As the unit progresses, you will teach children to return to their booklets to revise, revise, revise. At first, children's revisions will amount to little more than adding details—sometimes just to the picture—but across this unit you will teach qualities of good narrative writing. As youngsters learn more about good writing, they'll revise by drawing on that growing knowledge of qualities of good writing and of craft moves.

Why teach a unit on personal narrative writing at all? For starters, know that the founder of the writing process approach to writing, Pulitzer Prize–winning writer Donald Murray, always began his graduate school courses on writing by teaching aspiring writers that one's own lived experiences are worth cherishing through writing. Since then, it has been traditional for many writing workshop teachers to launch the year with a unit or two on personal narrative writing. The good news is that this decision is firmly rooted in the Common Core State Standards. The Common Core suggests that across the entire day and year, the amount of time students spend on information, opinion, and narrative writing should be equal. One can assume that the writing students do in social studies and science will tend to be information writing (and sometimes opinion writing), which means, then, that to ascribe to the tenants of the Common Core, it will be important for you to devote a good proportion of the writing classroom to narrative writing. For students to develop the ambitious skill levels that are described in the CCSS and illustrated in Appendix B of the Standards document, students will need not only to be taught the qualities of good narrative writing but also to have opportunities to practice narrative writing and receive feedback. The most accessible place to begin is with a unit on writing personal narratives.

Although the standards state that second-graders should be able to recount a well-elaborated event, including details, thoughts, actions, and feelings and provide a sense of closure, this little list of expectations doesn't come close to conveying what the pieces of writing in the appendix to the Common Core Standards convey. The message is clear: youngsters need to develop high-level skills in narrative writing. In this unit, then, children will learn that writers select small, meaningful moments from their lives and then write those as narratives across the pages of booklets.

If children come to your second grade with a backpack of tools for writing narrative in general, and Small Moment narrative writing in particular, you will probably bypass this unit and begin the year with *Lessons from the Masters*. If for some reason you elect to teach this unit to students who already have a repertoire of skills for writing Small Moment narratives, be sure to remind them to draw on that repertoire. Either way, your unit will need to guide your students toward meeting the CCSS for second-grade writers.

A SUMMARY OF THE BENDS IN THE ROAD FOR THIS UNIT

In Bend I (Teach Children to Write Lots of Focused, Simple, Small Moment Narratives Easily), students learn to easily write lots of focused, simple, Small Moment narratives. During this bend, you teach students strategies for choosing small moments from their lives so that they are able to generate ideas for stories quickly. Youngsters will be taught to think of a story idea, and then to sketch "twin sentences" about each thing. And then they'll learn to say the accompanying story aloud, and then to write it page by page. The entire process happens within one or two days of writing time, and students write a collection of stories during the first bend. As children become more experienced at writing narratives, you'll help them use all they know about personal narrative writing to plan the stories so that the stories written later in this bend are apt to be more focused, detailed, and lively. Plan to dedicate approximately a week and a half to this bend.

In Bend II (Teach Children to Write Longer, More Developed Stories), the stories your students write will become longer, more elaborated upon, and more fully developed. Graduate them to five-page booklets if you can, and rally them to write. They will continue to write many stories, applying all they are learning with increasing independence and skill. This should take about a week.

In Bend III (Revise), students engage in major revision work. Children first choose one of the many Small Moment stories they will have written and engage in major revision work with that one story. Then they'll return to other favorite pieces and revise those as well. Allow almost a week for this bend.

In Bend IV (Edit to Prepare for Publication), students learn to edit their work by editing the one piece of writing that each child chooses to publish. This bend will likely be short (only two days or so), ending with a publishing party during which students celebrate all the revision they attempted.

GETTING READY
Gather Texts for Students

To prepare for this unit, you may want to gather up a few books to read aloud outside of writing workshop to celebrate the writing process and inspire your students. Look for books such as Peter Reynolds's *Ish*; *The Best Story*, by Eileen Spinelli; or excerpts from *A Writer's Notebook*, by Ralph Fletcher. You can also gather examples of strong narrative writing that you might use as mentor texts in this unit. You'll find that generally, personal narratives have been altered into realistic fiction before they are published. You'll probably content yourself with studying realistic fiction that tells the story of a small moment or two. Mo Willems's *Knuffle Bunny* is a special favorite for this unit. The amount of text is sparse, making the book not altogether different from the sort of text second-graders can aspire to write. Ezra Jack Keats's *The Snowy Day* is another favorite, for similar reasons. Once you have chosen a mentor text or two, read that text aloud more than once and recruit children to talk about their favorite parts and about the decisions the author has made. By immersing children in a few mentor texts prior to and then during the unit, you give them wellsprings to draw on as they write.

Choose When and How Children Will Publish

For the first half of the unit, students will write and collect as many stories in their writing folder as they can. At the end of the second bend, you may decide to have a small writing celebration. You don't have to make a big deal of this. You might decide to dedicate the share portion of your last workshop in Bend II to this celebration, perhaps focusing on just one aspect of narrative writing—endings each student is particularly proud of or a child's favorite page. Then, in the third bend, children will choose first just one story on which to do major revision work and then several others if there's time. Of course, kids will have done some revision all along as they were continually rereading and adding to their drafts, but during the third bend, the children will learn how to do serious, heavy-duty revision. One revised piece from each child becomes the published personal narrative. Students will edit and proofread the selected pieces for

4

the final celebration. In the final celebration, perhaps the original version and the revised version of each published piece is displayed side by side.

BEND I: TEACH CHILDREN TO WRITE LOTS OF FOCUSED, SIMPLE, SMALL MOMENT NARRATIVES EASILY

Teach students to generate ideas.

On the very first day of the unit, you'll need to talk up the joys of writing and lure children to think of true stories and then to put these onto the pages of little booklets. Perhaps the best way to lure children into writing is to act as if *of course* they'll be dying to do this, as you are, and to act as if thinking up a true story and getting that story onto the pages of a book will be no big deal. We're assuming you've chosen to teach this unit rather than *Lessons from the Masters* because your children have not participated in a personal narrative writing workshop prior to now, or if they have, that experience wasn't one you want to build on, so you probably will feel best if you launch the year by teaching students a strategy for coming up with ideas for true stories. Start simple. Don't worry, for now, about whether students' ideas are especially focused. For example, you might teach students that to come up with ideas for writing true stories, writers start by thinking about the things they do. They come up with a few true stories of things they do, then choose one to write.

Having taught a strategy, you'll want to demonstrate that strategy—and demonstrate how easy it is to go from thinking of a topic to sketching the story out across pages. "I've been thinking about what I've done lately. The things that a person does can be made into good stories. For example, I could write about when I bought new shoes yesterday, or about going out for pizza last night. Yes! That's it. I'll write about going out for pizza." Notice that in this example, my story ideas were all focused Small Moment stories (don't take the notion of a Small Moment story too literally; these tend to be twenty-minute stories, not literally one small moment), but notice, too, that I did not make a big deal of this. The first goal is to get writers generating story ideas easily and moving immediately toward writing.

You'll also want to show writers that once a writer thinks of a story idea, it helps to plan out how that idea can be told as a story that unfolds bit by bit across pages. The fact that a story is told bit by bit—sequentially—is a fundamental part of writing a narrative, so bring that idea into the very start of the unit. I'd touch each page of a three-page (or five-page, if students are more advanced) booklet and then say aloud the story I planned to write. My story might start, "We ordered a large pizza with pepperoni." I'd draw the fastest possible sketch, and then I'd move to telling the next thing that happened in the plot line of the event. "I ate three pieces, my sister ate two."

If my students were very new to a writing workshop, and I thought that for today, they'd probably write fairly bare-bones stories, I'd then move to saying aloud the conclusion. "It was delicious. Then we had dessert, and ate and ate until we were full." In that one minilesson, I presumably wouldn't have time to draw or write those final two pages, but I'd let children know that's what I did do next, and that they should do so as well.

At the end of that first minilesson, I might record the strategy that I'd taught that day on a chart titled "Strategies for Generating Narrative Writing." A word of caution: any strategy, by definition, involves a step-by-step procedure. So the items on your chart can't be topics (people, places, and so on) but instead need to be procedures. "Think of something you do, then think what happens first, next, next; then stretch it across pages."

That first day, then, children will think of story ideas, draw each across the pages of a small booklet, and then write as best they can, telling what happened first, then next, and then next. Throughout the rest of the bend, students will continue writing something like a booklet a day.

In one of your early minilessons, you might teach another strategy or two for generating ideas. You might suggest that when writers do not know what to write about, they sometimes think about times they are dying to tell other kids about and write about those times. Teach your children that this process is quick. They should take only a few minutes to think of a great time they had, or a terrible time, and then remember what happened at the beginning and after that. This process of brainstorming ideas for writing encompasses a minute or so, nothing more. Then, too, you might teach kids that they can think of things they do a lot and come up with one particular time they did that thing. "All the time, my brother and I fight over who has the remote control of the TV. I'll tell about one time we had that fight."

Remember, too, that in just one day you can lay out several possible strategies for generating writing. You might demonstrate one in the minilesson, another in your mid-workshop teaching, and one more in your share.

Of course, once you have taught several strategies for generating true story ideas, these all go on your chart, and you'll encourage students to draw from any one of these strategies on any given day. The last thing you want is to teach a minilesson about one particular strategy for writing true stories and then expect each writer to put into motion only the strategy you have just taught. Instead, you will want to emphasize that writers always draw on all they have ever learned. It is important that children are able to use and reuse their small repertoire of strategies with independence. So take a count one day. How many of your kids are using the strategy you taught that day? Hopefully less than half! How many are drawing on strategies they learned on previous days or on ones they have invented? If most of your class routinely does only whatever you talk about in that day's minilesson, you'll want to lend your full weight toward reminding writers to draw on their *full* repertoire of strategies.

Teach students strategies to lift the level of their stories: sequence and focus.

Remember that for any minilesson you teach your students, you'll want to have a pocketful of coaching tips in mind that you might teach during your conferences, small groups, mid-workshop teachings, and shares. For example, you might want to teach children that it is important to start a story by telling what happened first, not by telling all about it. If a child begins a story about fighting over the remote control by writing, "Last night my brother and I fought about the remote control as always, and I won," it won't be easy to build a sequential, well-ordered tale from that beginning. On the other hand, it will be easy to write a well-ordered, sequential story if the tale starts, "My brother asked me, 'Where's the remote?' I hid it under the sofa pillow, but I said, 'I don't know.'"

As the days go by, you'll want to teach students to write focused stories. We have found it helpful to teach writers that instead of writing about "watermelon" ideas, they can write "small seed" stories. Instead of writing about "my trip to the zoo," the writer zooms in and writes just about feeding an elephant. You can't emphasize enough the importance of writing in detail and sequence. Stories depend on both, and your youngsters will be much stronger writers if they continue to tell and write their narratives with attention to these two basic elements.

Teach students strategies to lift the level of their stories: envisioning.

During these first days of the unit, you will also want to teach writers that between the time they choose a small moment to turn into a story and the time they start writing, they need to do one crucial thing: they need to dream the dream of the story and remember what happened so they can put the story onto the page. That is, they need to relive the moment, bit by bit, re-creating exactly what they did and said and thought. This takes some fictionalizing, because most people don't usually remember every precise detail of moments in the past. Steer children to think, "Okay, where was I, exactly? What was I doing, exactly?"

Of course, once a young writer pictures what he or she was doing, it will help if the writer quickly sketches that onto the page. Some children will tend to want to draw everything from the sun and clouds in the sky to the individual blades of grass, so you'll want to coach these students to draw just the main things they remember happening. Tell them, "Right now you just want to use sketching to capture the main things that happened. Then you can come back and write the whole story of each part."

As you teach sequence, focus, and envisioning, also support independence.

As you teach students qualities that make for more effective stories, you may find that they become a bit less sure of themselves as writers. The expectations are rising; the stories that kids around them are telling and writing will be more detailed, easier to imagine—in short, better. Some students will probably say to you, "I don't know what to write about. I don't have any good ideas."

If that happens, celebrate the fact that children are not just grabbing any ol' idea and writing about it. The truth is that some things a person does will make for better stories than other things, and it is wise of young writers to begin thinking whether the kids will like a story about eating Cheerios. Although there will be good aspects to any onset of writer's block, you'll also want to teach writers strategies for getting past writer's block so they can continue to be enormously productive during writing time. You might, for example, teach them that if they are stuck for ideas, they can refer to the chart, which lists the strategies you have taught thus far.

Notice that a chart for getting ideas lists *strategies*, as in actions the student can take, rather than content or topics to write about. One strategy might be to think about things that you do, choose one, and remember what happened first and then next. Another might be to think about things you are dying to tell the other kids. These are strategies, not topics.

It is impossible to overemphasize the importance of teaching writers that before writing, writers first make movies in their minds of how their story might go. If a child talks "all about" an event—if a child summarizes it with sentences such as, "It was a good baseball game. We won 6 to 2. I got a lot of hits. It was exciting."—then the child is *commenting on* the game rather than *telling the story* of it. The child has not yet grasped the idea of writing in a storyteller's voice. If, on the other hand, his piece begins, "I grabbed a bat and walked up to the plate. I looked at the pitcher and said, 'I'm ready,'" then the child is writing a story. Most children need to be reminded to make movies in their minds and to write so that readers can picture exactly what is happening.

As children become more fluent, raise the bar (one way to do this is by reminding children to pay attention to conventions).

Your children will be writing rough drafts, and writers never expect rough drafts to be perfect. There will be a time before the writing is published for children to make sure that their drafts represent their best work.

However, just because children are writing rough drafts doesn't mean you want them to throw all concern for convention to the wind. You'll want to coach children to take an extra minute to do what has almost, but not quite, become automatic for them. For example, if children aren't writing with ending punctuation, tell them that by second grade, writers do this. They may not punctuate correctly, but they should be writing with ending punctuation and with capitals, too.

Notice, too, whether children have a repertoire of about a hundred high-frequency words that they always spell correctly. If you are questioning, "Why emphasize conventions so early on in the unit?"—if you are thinking, "Shouldn't editing wait until the end of the process?"—then you are well schooled in writing workshop methodologies. And it is true that this isn't a time to worry whether students' spelling is perfect. But that doesn't mean that writers should place zero attention on conventions; certainly one would expect that the first-draft writing that second-graders produce is a lot more conventional than the first-draft writing first-graders produce! You will want to coach your second-graders by saying, "You are in second grade now. You should be spelling 'said' correctly every time you write. Push yourself to do that."

Of course, not all students will come to you demonstrating command of conventions, but if some of your students are not working at grade-level expectations, you will want to spend some time bringing them up to speed. For example, if your students come to you expecting that punctuation is something writers add just before a piece is published, you can teach them that writers write with punctuation all the time. Periods aren't an add-on, inserted just prior to publication! Teach students who do not have the instinct to punctuate that when writers have a thought, they write that thought without pausing (not writing word by word) and then put a period at the end of it. Then, the writer generates the next thought, writes that thought down all in a rush, and punctuates that thought.

Then, too, encourage children to write with some sense for when they have misspelled a word. Encourage the child who is unsure of a spelling to underline or circle the word and perhaps to take a second to try spelling it another way. Once a writer has taken an extra few seconds to work on the spelling of a particular word, it is best to move on. This is not the time of year to make a big deal out of spelling perfectly, to bring rough-draft writing to a halt for ten minutes while students check each word. This *is* the time of year to emphasize fluency, drafting quickly, taking a moment to spell correctly words that children can probably figure out, using the word wall as a quick reference, and moving on, rereading to edit *as best they can*. There will be time prior to publication to return to words that may not be spelled correctly.

By the end of the first bend, students will have written about half a dozen true stories. If this was their first workshop on personal narrative writing, it is likely that many of them will have written fairly brief bare-bones stories, perhaps with a few sentences on a page and perhaps with just three pages in a booklet. Others, of course, will have written more elaborate stories.

BEND II: TEACH CHILDREN TO WRITE LONGER, MORE DEVELOPED STORIES
Teach children to write much longer stories and to story-tell as a way to rehearse.

This next bend of the unit is an opportunity to teach children to elaborate in ways that bring stories to life. You might start by telling children that the goal of the upcoming bend will be to write much longer stories. You can provide longer booklets that contain more lines, although you will presumably still want to differentiate paper. Perhaps booklets for some of the children are full size and some are smaller. The small size is often especially popular, so this is a way to differentiate without making anyone feel bad.

Of course, once you have told children that your hope is that they will write a lot more and you've given them paper on which they can do so, you'll want to give them some strategies for writing more. Perhaps the most important strategy you can teach is that of storytelling a story prior to writing it. Storytelling prior to writing can help young writers write with more voice and volume. We find it works for children to touch the page on which they plan to write and story-tell just the part of the story that will go on that page. This allows them to story-tell bit by bit, just as you are hoping they'll write. You might take this further and teach them that the part of their story on each page will have a beginning, a middle, and an end. So instead of page one being, "We went to the pizza restaurant," you'll be coaching the child to say, "Mom and Dad and me drove to the pizza restaurant. When we got there, the parking lot smelled like pizza. We hurried into the restaurant."

You might teach children that writers often find lots of people who will listen to a story, and they tell the story multiple times, making it better each time. You might provide some of the goals for this storytelling. You might say, "Try to story-tell in a way that gives your partner goose bumps," or "Try, this time, to stretch out the good parts, really making them into a big deal," or, "Think about how you want your listener to feel at the start of the story, and tell the start to get your listener feeling that way. *Then* think how you want your listener to feel later in the story, and tell that part in a way that gets your listener feeling that way."

Teach children to start a story with a good lead. This makes it more likely that the story will be sequential and detailed.

As children story-tell, you might tweak their oral stories in ways that lift the level of those stories and give children tips for doing this themselves. One of the most important things you might do is help children get off to a good start. Usually stories are better if they start closer to the main action. A story about catching a fish need not begin with waking up the day of fishing. Instead, it can begin with threading the worm onto the hook or with casting. Notice that although this action doesn't require a prolonged buildup before the main event of catching a fish, it *is* an initiating action. Remember that it is very characteristic of a young child to want to get to the main thing right from the start. The story will probably end up being confusing if the first page says, "One day I caught a great big fish" and only then goes back to the starting action!

Teach writers to tell the story bit by bit.

One of the best ways for children to elaborate is to tell more details about what happens in their stories, and to do this, you'll want to help children tell and write their stories in smaller steps so that they write in a more bit-by-bit fashion. You can illustrate this by pacing out a story across your classroom floor. If the story is told in giant steps and it is a Small Moment story, it won't last long. "We drove to the pizza restaurant. We ordered pizza. We ate it." That same story can be told in smaller steps.

"My mom asked, 'Do you want to go out for pizza?' and I danced around the kitchen, excited. The drive there was quick and the whole time I thought about the kind of pizza I would order. When we got to the pizza shop, the whole parking lot smelled like pizza."

Children can ask themselves questions: "What was I doing? What exactly? What did I say?" If they learn to ask themselves these questions as they write, they will become more independent in including details that bring a story to life.

Teach children that a partner can help them write more elaborated stories.

Show students that partners can help them write much more elaborated stories. Writers can story-tell and act out stories for their partners prior to writing them. They can use partners as listeners who ask questions and who let writers know the kinds of questions that readers will have. If midway through a writing workshop children sit hip to hip with a partner, the two partners reading first one writer's book and then the other's and talking together about the questions readers will have and the details the writer can add, it is far more likely that children will write a paragraph on a page, not just a sentence! The truth is that almost any goal can be supported by partner work, as long as you channel partners to provide that support.

As stories become longer, remind children that caring about conventions should not be postponed.

Chances are, your students will need reminders to use some of the basic conventions so that these become part of their everyday writing process. Routine reminders help children develop the habit of writing with ending punctuation and starting sentences with capitals; you'll certainly want that. It can also help to use mid-workshop teaching points as a vehicle for reminding children to use the word wall to help them spell sight words conventionally or to remind children that during the last minutes of the workshop, it helps to reread one's work to check for conventions and spelling patterns.

Some children in your class will probably write without a lot of concern for spelling, while others will obsess about every word, wanting your seal of approval for every decision. Be sure to differentiate your instruction, helping the free-flowers take that extra second to remember to write in lowercase letters (unless uppercase is called for) and to pause to spell word wall words correctly. Meanwhile, help those children who see writing as little more than an exercise in spelling and penmanship to focus on content, and to write quickly and fluently. Remember that rough-draft writing is not supposed to be perfect, but that as children grow more experienced as writers, more and more writing skills can and will become automatic and effortless for them.

BEND III: REVISE

Generate excitement for the most important writing work of all: revision.

During this bend, I recommend that you teach writers the importance of revision. Some children think of revision as a punishment for bad writing—you'll want, instead, to talk about revision as a way to honor one's best writing. Encourage children to reread all they have written and to select their best writing to revise, perhaps moving that writing into a special revision folder. To add to the drum roll, you might say, "Today is going to be a very special day. Today, you will begin to do the most important writing work of all. You'll be *revising*." Of course, all of your kids will have been revising, to some extent, all along, but you'll be suggesting that there is a deeper kind of revision as well. Then teach students a number of lenses they can use to reread, rethink, and revise their best writing. These ways to revise a piece of writing will need to be collected on a chart, because before the unit is over, you'll suggest that, in fact, writers draw from this repertoire of revision strategies whenever they write and revise.

Once each child has selected a piece of writing that he or she wants to revise, you may want to make a photocopy of each child's original draft. That way, when you publish the revised writing at the end of the unit, you can put the two pieces side by side and allow students to reflect on the growth and changes to their writing that came through all their hard revision work.

Teach children to revise by adding detail to their texts.

Now you'll begin teaching the various lenses for revision. You might start with something extra easy and appealing. Earlier in the unit, you emphasized that sketching could be used as a tool for planning quickly. Now you might return to sketching, this time suggesting it can be a tool for revision. You might teach kids that writers often reread, thinking, "What else do I remember? What else could I add to my story?"

Once kids have revised to add more detail to their pictures, you might teach them to revise by adding more to their accompanying text as well. The goal, of course, can't just be to "add more." You'll think of ways to rally children to understand the importance of elaboration. Perhaps you'll talk about the fact that readers want to be able to picture what really happened, in which case you'll talk up the importance of details that let readers know what things were really like. "You said that you had pizza, but readers won't know what the pizza was like. Can you tell me about it?" Once a child has told you about the pizza, be sure that you not only encourage the youngster to add the tasty detail to the draft. You can go far, teaching students a kind of thing that can be added first to pictures, then to their writing. For example, chances are good that there was no setting to the original pictures. "Show the place where this happened," you can say. You can then encourage writers to add details about the setting throughout their story. You could suggest other sorts of additions: defining features of the characters, for example.

A few words of caution: Earlier I pointed out that after teaching kids strategies for generating narrative writing, you want to be sure your teaching gives kids a repertoire from which they draw, and I cautioned you to guard against spooning out one strategy at a time and expecting each writer to use that one strategy in sync. The same is true here. In one minilesson, you can suggest a few possible ways narrative writers can add to their sketches and their written texts, and then expect children to make choices.

Then, too, know that adding details leads to mixed results. The truth is that in the end, you'll want writers to write with these details rather than using carets or "spider leg flags" to stick in little add-ons. It is okay, however, if the product isn't perfect. The work of recalling more and elaborating more develops essential muscles.

This week, you can teach writing other revision strategies as well. If children are not yet incorporating direct dialogue into their stories, you will find it is magical to teach them that they can add talk, or direct address, to their stories. Teach them that it helps to insert the exact words that a character (probably the child) is apt to have said. Of course, the process of adding dialogue needs to begin with recalling the event, so you'll probably demonstrate by showing children that when you do this, you start by making a movie in your mind, and then you remember (or imagine) what each person said.

Again, you'll want to record the strategies you teach on your chart, "Strategies for Revising Narrative Writing."

Teach children that focus also counts. Writers revise by subtracting.

After suggesting that writers can revise by recalling an event, then adding details to a sketch of it and to the written account and also writers to add direct address, you might next teach students that writers reread not just to add details but also to make sure that their stories are focused. Kids might reread, asking themselves, "Is this still the same small moment?"

Sometimes we have literally told students that as important as adding is in revision, subtracting, too, can be important. And the most important things to subtract are the bits of a story that turn what was meant to be a Small Moment story into an unfocused story. Usually when I want to make a point, I use an exaggerated example. I might, for instance, create a rambling addition to the pizza story, adding a final page that tells about returning home, feeding the dog, and then watching a TV show. Then I could recruit the class to join me in seeing whether I may now need to subtract.

There are some hints that usually help a child be aware of ways in which a Small Moment story has lost its focus. If the setting has totally changed from one page to the next, chances are the story is also moving from one scene to another, and usually that new scene won't be integral to the first.

Then, too, if the story is titled "A Pizza Supper" and there are parts that have nothing to do with pizza, that's a clue that those parts may need to be subtracted.

Of course, in time you will teach children that a story is often constructed of two or even three scenes (and small moments) but for many second-graders, writing long stories that are also focused is not easy. The two goals—focus and length—seem to the youngster to be contradictory. For now, it is important to help youngsters know that the entire five-page booklet should tell the story of one small moment. Do not be surprised if you find yourself teaching kids to "zoom in on one small moment" or "narrow down" their stories again and again. With practice, many examples, coaching, feedback, and lots of opportunity to approximate, you will see kids make great strides. The resulting story will be detailed and lively.

Sometimes, the subtracting that is called for will be to help moderate excessive additions children included as part of revision. When you encourage youngsters to add dialogue to a story, it is not unusual for the stories to become swamped with dialogue. Readers often can't even discern who is speaking or what is happening. When you see this sort of writing, keep in mind that the child is probably making movies in his mind, which is a great thing, but you might still let children know that adding talk is like adding salt—do so in moderation.

Provide physical tools to create new energy.

When teaching youngsters to revise by adding and subtracting from their drafts, you will need to see to it that children have the tools to do this work. Scissors and tape will matter. When teaching youngsters to add to a draft, you'll need to show them that they can literally scissor apart a draft, inserting half sheets of paper that act as expanders. Show them that they can tape spider legs onto the margins of a draft to give themselves room to grow. Then, too, show children that the pages of a book can be taken out—thrown away or packaged into a second book. The good news about this physical sort of work is that children love to make spider legs and flaps, to take booklets apart and reorder the pages. The "carpentry" of revision will lure youngsters to do this work.

You might introduce a special revision pen in a new color, perhaps purple, so that kids' revisions will stand out from their original work. You and your students will be able to assess, at a glance, their "before" work in black and the "after" revisions in purple. Revising in a new color also allows you to see, at a glance, who in your class is struggling with revision (i.e., there's no purple on the page), so that you can gather those youngsters in a small group for extra support.

Meanwhile, there will be another physical dimension to this. Once children have revised one piece well, you'll want to encourage them to reread all their writing and choose another piece or two that they especially like, putting that second and perhaps that third piece into their revision folder where it, too, can be revised.

Rally energy around revision by asking children to act and then revise.

Once you have taught children to add to their best draft and subtract from it as well, and you have helped children know some things that can be added or subtracted, you'll want to decide whether your unit would benefit from an infusion of new instruction, designed to ramp up students' energy for revision. If children have selected a few more stories that are good enough to merit revision, you may decide to show them yet more ways to revise. One of the best, most exciting ways for children to revise narratives is for them to dramatize their writing, using the performance as a way to elaborate. There's nothing like a performance to show children what's missing in a story. A writer and his or her partner could read a bit of the writer's text aloud, then act out what that bit says (not what the author wishes it said!), and then read the next bit, acting out that bit as well. Chances are, the actors will quickly realize things that have been left out. "No, you need to do this!" one will say, followed by the specific observation. This kind of dramatizing is a surefire way to highlight for children the fundamental concept that narratives include movement; they have action, dialogue, and gestures that lift characters off the page and onto a (mental) stage. Your children will have fun fleshing out their pieces with more interaction between characters, with bigger, bolder responses and more lively action.

Your challenge, meanwhile, will be to guide children to unleash their imaginations while remaining grounded in the stories they are trying to tell. If an overly eager partner introduces suggestions that don't match the writer's vision, you'll want to gently intercept and get these two back on track. Acting can be a terrific way to get at the conflict, the drama of a story, but with young children you may need to do some reining in. You might coach children to ask the right questions as they elaborate: "What exactly did that look like?" "What happened next?" "What did she say back?" "How did you feel? How can you show that on your face? With your body?" And so on.

Teach writers to try out different leads and endings.

Another way you might teach children to revise their work is by helping them give careful thought to how they both begin and end their stories. A stronger lead often leads to a stronger story, so you might teach students to try out new leads for their existing story. A student might try out three different leads, writing each possibility on a strip of paper, and then choose the best one and tape it into her book. Often, once a child has revised the lead to her story, she may also want to reconsider her ending. You might show them a few mentor texts with different types of endings. For example, Kevin Henkes's *A Box of Treats* stories all end with dialogue or a thought. Mo Willems ends *Knuffle Bunny* with a take-away that lets the reader know what about the story was important: "And those were the first words Trixie ever spoke."

However kids decide to end their stories, the key in this bend is that they *try out different endings*. It is the process of rethinking and reconsidering an existing draft that is the goal in this unit, not simply writing one decent ending the first time through and leaving it without consideration of other possibilities. Be prepared for the reality that in the process of trying out new endings, some children might choose an ending that makes the overall story *worse*, and know that over time, as kids get more and more feedback and chances to share their writing, they will become wiser and more experienced at making those decisions.

Teach the qualities of good writing.

As you teach children to revise, you will be teaching them about the qualities of good writing, because always, revisions need to be efforts to make writing better—to add more of what works and to take away what doesn't work. You will certainly want students to self-assess often and to use the checklist for narrative writing as a guide for their revisions. You will probably want to show your children not just the checklist for second grade but also the one for third grade, because a knowledge of the next steps can inform what your writers do—and they'll *love* to do "third-grade work"! The Narrative Writing Checklist, Grades 2 and 3 can be found on the CD-ROM.

You, also, will use a checklist to guide *your* work. You should be able to check off that yes, you are teaching students to introduce a narrator (the children will be showing themselves acting in ways that reveal

Narrative Writing Checklist

	Grade 2	NOT YET	STARTING TO	YES!	Grade 3	NOT YET	STARTING TO	YES!
	Structure				**Structure**			
Overall	I wrote about *one time* when I did something.	☐	☐	☐	I told the story bit by bit.	☐	☐	☐
Lead	I thought about how to write a good beginning and chose a way to start my story. I chose the action, talk, or setting that would make a good beginning.	☐	☐	☐	I wrote a beginning in which I helped readers know who the characters were and what the setting was in my story.	☐	☐	☐
Transitions	I told the story in order by using words such as *when, then,* and *after*.	☐	☐	☐	I told my story in order by using phrases such as *a little later* and *after that*.	☐	☐	☐
Ending	I chose the action, talk, or feeling that would make a good ending.	☐	☐	☐	I chose the action, talk, or feeling that would make a good ending and worked to write it well.	☐	☐	☐
Organization	I wrote a lot of lines on a page and wrote across a lot of pages.	☐	☐	☐	I used paragraphs and skipped lines to separate what happened first from what happened later (and finally) in my story.	☐	☐	☐
	Development				**Development**			
Elaboration	I tried to bring my characters to life with details, talk, and actions.	☐	☐	☐	I worked to show what happened to (and in) my characters.	☐	☐	☐
Craft	I chose strong words that would help readers picture my story.	☐	☐	☐	I not only told my story, but also wrote it in ways that got readers to picture what was happening and that brought my story to life.	☐	☐	☐

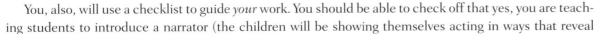

who they are). Yes, children will be organizing an event sequence that unfolds naturally. Yes, they will use dialogue and descriptions of actions, and chances are they will need lots of instruction and practice in doing this well.

The checklist may remind you of some items you've forgotten to teach. For example, it may nudge you to remember to teach your kids to use time markers to show the sequence of events, including such words and phrases as *later* or *after that*. You may also want to show a few of your more advanced writers some of the sophisticated ways authors show the passage of time. "The sky was growing dark by the time our team bus pulled into the parking lot," or "I glanced at my cell phone and saw we were late."

All of these qualities of good writing are must-haves for narratives, so before wrapping up the unit, we suggest you ask your kids to check over their own writing (and perhaps their writing partner's), to see what they have and haven't done. Then they can set some goals to work toward for the last day or so of the unit, so that they each have one last chance to incorporate everything that a strong narrative piece of writing should contain.

BEND IV: EDIT TO PREPARE FOR PUBLICATION

Remind students to use the conventions they already know.

With an author's celebration just around the bend, you'll want to let children know that they need to choose their one best piece from the unit to publish. Then you can help them edit that piece carefully. You will presumably already have a word wall featuring high-frequency words that you have taught explicitly. If you haven't done so already, teach your children that writers reread, checking to be sure they use word wall words correctly. These are, after all, the words that the class has already studied together.

You will also want to remind children, once again, that they need to be sure they have written with periods and capitals to signal the endings and beginnings of sentences. This concept is not a simple one, and you can teach it without children mastering it. Help your writers understand that writers think of a sentence as a thought, write that thought down in a rush, then add the period at the end of the thought. Then they think of the next thought and begin to write it using a capital letter.

After your students fix some spelling and punctuation in their stories, the pieces will probably still be far from correct. You may want to call children into small groups to teach them one more thing. Some might benefit from learning about commas and quotation marks, others from learning the spelling of a common word ending. Do they capitalize names of people, places, and titles? Whatever the conventions, once children learn them, they need to incorporate them into the draft they hope to publish (and of course they can get additional practice by rereading their other work and fixing these aspects of their other stories as well).

Teach spelling strategies that can be applied to student writing.

Check also to see whether your children spell polysyllabic words by stretching them out, saying them slowly, and representing every syllable and sound they hear. If they do, encourage them to remember that once they have voiced a syllable—for instance, *tion*—they will want to think, "What other *-tion* words do I know? How can I use the words I know to help me spell this word that I don't know?" That is, children need to progress from relying on sound alone toward relying on analogy (and on their knowledge of spelling patterns).

Develop a class chart of conventions that students should be responsible for in their writing. Once you've taught how to capitalize titles, for instance, this capitalization must become an expectation for the writing kids do every day, across the day, in all subjects. This way, your editing instruction can focus on a new goal during the next round of publication.

You will, of course, have a separate time in your day for word study, and during that time you will no doubt teach children some high-frequency words, especially the commonly misspelled high-frequency words. To decide on the words to teach, get a list of high-frequency words (Pat Cunningham's book, *What Really Matters in Vocabulary: Research-Based Practices across the Curriculum* (2008), is one source for this list) and notice which words many writers do not seem to have mastered yet. Start with those! The word wall is not a place for new and fancy vocabulary or for social studies words. It is a place for the high-frequency or high-utility words that you plan to teach and then hold children accountable for always spelling correctly.

You don't need to get overly invested in making published pieces perfect. Presumably you are teaching this unit is at the start of your year, so your goal is certainly not perfection. These are little kids and their work will not be perfect. If you are publishing student writing within the four walls of your classroom, most teachers would agree that it is entirely okay to publish work that represents the children's best, not your best. If, on the other hand, you plan to hang the student writing in the hall and your school expects pieces displayed in the hallway to be correct, you might see whether you can recruit some parents to type up students' work after they have done lots of editing and made the piece the best it can be. That is, if you feel the work needs to be perfect, don't use children's time to make it so. You'd ultimately need to correct each piece of writing yourself for the writing to be perfect, and asking children to recopy your corrections is not really a rigorous way for children to spend their time. It would be far more rigorous for you to ask them to write something new (perhaps an "about the author" page) and to do this writing showing that all the things they learned to do during editing have now become part of their first-draft writing.

We want to caution you against doing too much to prop up student's drafts of their work. If you spend a lot of time whispering in their ears what to do or making correct pages for them to recopy, then your students' work will not represent what your children can do independently at this early point in the year. This means that later, you and others will not be able to look at the progression of published pieces to see ways children have grown. Think of their first published pieces as their baseline, and don't make it entirely misleading by injecting too much of your writing abilities into their work.

Publish the writing through a celebration of the writing process.

This unit's publishing celebration can center around the writing process. Perhaps as part of the celebration you'll display a photocopy of each child's original booklet right next to their revised copy, with all the purple pen notations visible and the flaps taped onto that revised draft. One possibility is to mount the two pieces side by side on a large sheet of colored construction paper, and then spread the displays of writing around the room to create a "writing museum." Maybe you'll invite guests for this celebration, or maybe not. You might start the party by asking kids to talk with their writing partner about what they notice about each other's original draft and their new, revised draft. You can support their reflection by modeling: "I used to think . . . But now I know . . ." Or "In my old draft . . . But in my new draft . . ." There are other ways, of course, for students to reflect. Perhaps you'll ask kids to come to the meeting area with their on-demand assessments or their first piece of writing from the school year in hand, or maybe you'll gather them close and tell them the story of how the unit went, reminding them of each of the lessons, maybe sharing an example of student work from each day of the unit.

Following a bit of reflection, you might sing a favorite class song or read a writing-related poem. Perhaps you'll reread one of the books from the beginning of the year that inspired your kids as writers. Then you'll let your kids move around the room reading one another's work. Next to each display, kids can write compliments to their classmates on a compliment sheet that can be attached to the display following the celebration.

Take the time during the publishing celebration of this unit to help your writers take pride in all they have completed! Consider placing their pieces where any child in the school can read the work—in the library or on the bulletin board in the hallway (include a banner announcing that your class focused on revision with flaps and strips). Also help students reflect on and self-assess how much they have grown.

Finally, after or before that publication celebration, you'll want to give children a chance to do another on-demand assessment so they—and you—can see how much they've grown. Use the same prompt as you used for the original on-demand so that you can compare and contrast the work. Once they've written the new on-demand, show them how they can use the checklist to guide their self-assessment. The *Writing Pathways: Performance Assessments and Learning Progressions, K–5*, can guide you as you help your children do that important work.

Information Books

Using Writing to Teach Others All about Our Favorite Topics

RATIONALE/INTRODUCTION

The Common Core State Standards expect that students will spend a third of their total writing time writing informational or explanatory texts. This expectation is not aimed specifically at language arts—at the writing workshop—but instead fits under a portion of the Common Core that emphasizes that all subjects provide opportunities for literacy learning. You'll absolutely want children to write information texts of all sorts during social studies and science.

But before you take writing across the curriculum, you will want to ramp up children's writing skills, and there are no better ways to do so than through writing units that are designed to accelerate students skills at that kind of writing. When planning a curriculum for your informational and explanatory writing units, you'll want to begin with units that are more accessible and progress over time to units that are more challenging.

Lab Reports and Science Books, the unit featured in the second-grade series, will be an absolute favorite for your students. It's an unusual unit for us, because it is a hybrid between a science unit and a writing unit. Students conduct actual scientific investigations about force and motion, and they use writing to plan for, record, and reflect on those investigations. Later they use all they learn from their work with force and motion to write all-about books that explore a topic related to force and motion. This is heady, exciting work, and your students will devour the unit with great enthusiasm.

However, it is also ambitious work. Although students with very emergent writing skills can handle *Lab Reports and Science Books*, it will take children with basic information writing skills far; it supports differentiation. Therefore, it is entirely possible you may decide to teach a more straightforward information unit first, turning to *Lab Reports and Science Books* only *after* children have had some basic experience writing all-about books. The unit detailed in this chapter lets you accomplish that goal. It is a bit more advanced than the first-grade all-about unit (*Nonfiction Chapter Books*), but it is less advanced than *Lab Reports and Science Books*.

During this unit, children will write books on self-selected topics about which they have some knowledge. They will also do a bit of research on these topics, incorporating new knowledge into what they already know. The theory is that by writing information books on topics of their own choosing, children are more apt to feel invested in the project and therefore more likely to write with voice and conviction. You may encourage students to consider writing some texts about especially interesting topics related to social studies or science units they studied earlier in the year or are currently studying outside writing workshop, but you will also want to convey that it is fine for youngsters to choose personal topics, such as studying the country in which they were born or Arabian horses or soccer.

Writing volume is an important goal in this unit, and for starters, this means children will write many information books. A second goal is that children begin to explore and learn about different ways of structuring nonfiction texts. As they move from one book to the next, you will want to encourage them to experiment with a variety of text structures, thinking about which one best conveys information about a given topic. As children learn more about text structures, they may return to a book they wrote earlier in the unit, rewriting it with a new structure. Ultimately, of course, it is up to children to decide how best to structure each book to teach others.

Regardless of the structure writers choose, in the interest of upholding your volume goal, you will want to keep paper choices ambitious. Provide children with booklets that contain lots of pages and lots of lines for writers to fill. Be clear that you expect a lot of writing. A question-and-answer book does not mean one question followed by a sentence for an answer but rather a question to hook the reader and then whole paragraphs of writing to answer the question and teach information to help readers understand the answer to the question.

Throughout the unit, you'll use mentor texts to help you teach and entice!

A SUMMARY OF THE BENDS IN THE ROAD FOR THIS UNIT

In Bend I (Write Information Books with Stamina, Volume, and Independence), students will write as many information books as they can. They'll choose topics based on their own interests, starting out by making a table of contents as a strategy for planning and then writing a page for each chapter. You'll be able to teach this in a week, as long as writing occurs every day.

In Bend II (Write with Elaboration: Study a Mentor Text to Make Information Books Longer and More Interesting), kids will learn that each chapter can be planned with more detail, making whole booklets for each chapter rather than a single page. They'll learn strategies for elaboration, such as using examples and comparison. They will also learn to write introductions and conclusions. Allow a week for Bend II.

In Bend III (Revise One Book and Conduct Research to Create an Expert Project), students will choose one of the many information books they have created and stick with that topic for the remainder of the unit. The work they do now will be referred to as their *expert project*. To do this project, youngsters will conduct simple research, gathering information from a variety of sources (artifacts, photographs, and books). Ultimately each child will create an expert project, which will consist of a book with many chapters on a topic or a collection of separate books on a topic. Plan to spend about a week and a half working in Bend III.

In Bend IV (Edit, Fancy Up, and Publish the Writing So That It Teaches in Clear and Exciting Ways), students will prepare to present their expert projects at an expert fair, to which guests will be invited to hear students present their work. Students will edit and publish their informational books, as well as prepare an oral presentation, complete with visual aids. It will take three or four days to wrap up the unit.

GETTING READY
Gather Texts for Students

This unit will require more than one mentor text, because you'll want to show children a variety of very simple, replicable text structures. For example, you may want one book that is organized in a question/answer format, one that contains many different genres within the spread of chapters, one that is essentially an elaborated list, and so on. As you gather and collect these texts, you'll want to take time to study them yourself, thinking about how you might use them to demonstrate various aspects of writing that you can imagine illuminating. For example, although you may select texts because of their varied structures, you will probably also want to use them to teach students about the different kinds of information writers include in information texts and so you'll want to take note if a text includes statistics, close-up pictures, or definitions tucked into parentheses. You will likely also want to use the mentor texts to teach about different options for starting and ending an information book. The books themselves will give you ideas for the teaching you will want to do. This way, you enter the unit with a repertoire of ways to teach children about the qualities of this genre of writing.

Choose When and How Children Will Publish

You may decide to publish a book from Bends I and II and then hold a larger publication celebration at the end of the entire unit. Then again, you may decide to only hold the end-of-the-unit celebration. That choice is up to you.

At the end of the unit, I imagine that you might want to organize an expert fair, perhaps setting up a dozen little booths in the gym or a hallway, with one of your young experts manning each booth and teaching two or three "students" at a time who want to learn about the topic. By this final publication celebration, each child will have written either a small collection of books on his or her expert topic or one larger informational book with many well-developed chapters. The chapters and/or collection of books will represent a range of text structures. Some students might incorporate a how-to chapter (or book) or a narrative informational chapter (or book) in their project.

BEND I: WRITE INFORMATION BOOKS WITH STAMINA, VOLUME, AND INDEPENDENCE

Get started writing information books. Look at mentor texts and think about your own expertise.

As you think about how to launch this unit, consider this: young children tend to be fascinated by the world around them. They also are eager to dive into the work that older kids and grown-ups do. You can harness this, inviting them to write books that are similar to their favorite published information books. Once children learn that each of these books offers a sort of course on a topic, they will be all the more enthralled with the unit. Kids love to be experts, and they love to teach.

If most of your students wrote information books in first grade, you'll want to start the unit by reminding them that during the preceding year, they wrote lots of books on topics of their choice. Remind them, too, that the books they wrote included chapters. Then tell them that for the next five weeks they are going to extend all that they learned in order to write information books like the pros.

Of course, if many of your children didn't write information books during first grade, you'll need to set up the unit differently. You'll probably want to rely on some beautiful familiar information books that you have read aloud to your class, and use these as mentor texts—texts that your students can emulate. Choose one or two simple information books that teach "all about" a topic. Bobbie Kalman's *Hamsters* and other books in that series are great mentor texts for second-graders. National Geographic's *Animals* series, including *Pandas*, by Anne Schreiber, are also great examples of published information books. These are very much like the books your students will create in this unit. Show students the sorts of things you imagine they'll be doing. If this is utterly new to your children, you might start them off writing "teaching books" that don't have chapters but that set out to teach readers all about something the writer knows well—Legos, dogs, baby sisters. Within a few days, you could then graduate your students to write with chapters.

Either way, you'll want to teach students to generate ideas by thinking about subjects they could teach others—subjects on which they have some life experience. You might say to kids, "Think of topics that you know a lot about—anything at all that you could teach other people *all about*. It could be a sport or a place or an interest. Thumbs up when you've thought of a topic you know a lot about." Be sure to emphasize to your students that they will all be picking their own topics (not writing about yours), and be sure you encourage them to write about high-interest topics. For now, expect that their topics will not require any research. Learning how to research a topic will come later—once they have already learned how to write an information book.

The truth is, most of your children will have no trouble at all coming up with their first topic, whether they decide on dinosaurs, Legos, soccer, or trees, so it won't be necessary to devote an entire minilesson to that decision. The first part of a minilesson could be that kids think up a topic and quickly tell their partner all about it, but then you can go on and teach the next steps that writers go through to get ready to write.

Teach kids to break topics into subtopics with a table of contents.

If you find that it is no big deal for most of the children to generate topics for writing, and if most of them have had some experience writing information books, you might go further in your initial minilesson and right from the start teach writers that once information writers have chosen a topic, the next thing they do is to plan how the book will go. One way to do that is to plan chapters by creating a table of contents. You might show them an example of a table of contents from your mentor text, saying, "This author probably made this table of contents first, to help her get her whole book planned out." Whether you decide to tuck instruction such as this into the very start of your unit or postpone it for a day, you will probably use your own information text as well as published mentor texts to show children different ways writers might divide a topic into subtopics.

Perhaps your own topic is goldfish. You might let kids know that you are thinking your chapters could tell about the daily life of your goldfish—what it eats, how it sleeps, its movement. After that, you could write more chapters—telling about baby goldfish in one chapter, growing goldfish in another, and old goldfish in yet another. That is, you will probably want to have a logical structure for your chapters, even though you won't expect that children will follow suit. Organizing information writing according to a logical structure is a fifth-grade expectation in the Common Core, so you won't want to make a big thing of it. But we can't imagine a good reason for *not* immersing children in some of the qualities of effective information writing from the start.

Many teachers provide special paper for the table of contents; the paper contains a line for the chapter title and a line for the page number next to it (the page numbers can be filled in later, when the book is nearly complete). To help children consider whether they actually have something to say for each chapter in their planned table of contents, you might ask them to touch the lines on their table of contents paper and write-in-the-air how the intended chapter might go. If the child can't think of content for a chapter, that's probably not a good plan. From very early in the unit, then, your kids will have learned how information writers decide on a topic and use a table of contents to plan their writing, and they will have already done a good deal of that work. Plan for children to write books in which they have a new page for each chapter, with a box on the top of the page for sketching what they know and lines for writing the information that goes in the chapter. Most second-graders can write a paragraph in each chapter.

Be ready to lead small groups and to teach strategies for those children struggling with topic choice.

If some children struggle to come up with topics for information books, you can address that in a small group. You might let the writers in that group know that there are some territories that writers often mine when they write information books. You might then list possible categories—sports, animals, places, people, and so on. Of course, the challenge is to zoom in on a particular example of each of these—a particular subtopic related to sports or to an animal. You might teach these writers that things in their environment can spark ideas for information books. For example, even the classroom schedule holds topics for information books. A child could pick any time of the day (e.g., art, recess, writing workshop, math) and make a book about it. Similarly, a writer might imagine going on a walk through his house, noticing all the places and objects that spark ideas for topics. Remember that the point of this unit isn't for children to pick the most glamorous topics. E. B. White has written whole essays on warts, chickens, and commas. No topic comes with ready-made interest. Instead, authors make a topic interesting.

Teach children to focus their topics and their chapters, lifting the level of their work.

Because children will write several information books during the first bend of the unit, you will be able to lift the level of their topic choice as the unit unfolds. One way to do this is to move toward an emphasis on focus. The topics kids choose when writing information books tend to be very broad, with subtopics that fit together loosely. For example, a child who is writing "All about School" might choose the writing workshop as one chapter, a best friend as a second, and the room arrangement as a third. Or she might write a book about school in which each chapter is the name of a different kid in her class. Congratulate students when they grasp the concept that information books are often structured with one overarching topic divided into smaller subtopics or categories.

You might teach students who are ready for more challenging work that a topic such as school is very broad, and just as writers zoom in on small moments when writing narratives, writers also find it helps to zoom in on focused topics when writing information pieces. Instead of writing a book about school, a child would be well advised to write the book about art class or even about making papier-mâché pigs in art class.

Of course, once a writer has chosen a focused topic, he or she needs to maintain that focus. Sometimes as kids start listing possible chapters, they stray outside the boundary of the focused topic. You might use your own information mentor text as an example, saying, "Let's check to see that all the chapters in my book fit with my main idea." Then demonstrate rereading the table of contents, one chapter title at a time, making sure that each fits with the overarching topic of the book.

Draft long and strong—and let the draft lead students to alter their plans.

As children begin drafting their chapters, one minilesson might involve teaching them to write each chapter quickly, as best they can, writing down all the information they know and then moving on. It is helpful for children to realize that what they are doing as they write an information book is teaching a class on a topic. Instead of storytelling as a way to prime the pump for writing, information writers sometimes take time to teach their topic to someone, allowing that opportunity to help them anticipate places where people will have questions, long for more detail, or want more examples.

In a minilesson, you might teach kids that they can rehearse for their writing by telling their partner what they plan to write on each page of their book, writing-in-the-air, as mentioned earlier. The listening partners' role is to make sure they understand what the writer has said. You might say, "The trick is, if you, the listener, can't understand what your partner just said, you should coach him. You can say, 'Can you say that again?' or 'Can you explain what you mean?' or 'What did you really mean by that?'" The simple experience of being asked to clarify is helpful to young writers; it also fosters strong speaking and listening on the part of both the writer and the listener.

Of course, children needn't warm up for writing by teaching another person. Writers might also write-in-the-air, saying aloud to themselves what they intend to write before writing it, long and strong.

You might also help children use drawing to prime the pump for a chapter. In a minilesson, you might teach students to draw everything they know that fits with the chapter title using those sketches as a sort of visual planning sheet. For example, in a chapter on football equipment, the author might sketch the football field, the stadium, and all the equipment that the players wear.

Sometimes, as children do this, they discover that they need to turn one chapter into several chapters. For example, the one chapter on football equipment could be subdivided into many: there could be a whole chapter just on the gear that football players wear and another chapter on the football field. This strategy also works the other way around. If there isn't much to draw, then it might be difficult to write an entire chapter on the subtopic. Once children have drawn everything they know about a particular chapter, they then incorporate everything from the drawing into the words they write on the lines below the drawing. They can reread their writing, double-checking to see whether everything in the picture is also in the words.

Remind children to incorporate features of nonfiction books into their texts.

As you near the end of the first bend in the unit, children will be writing their second or more likely their third information book, and you will probably want to remind them of some of the features of information books. You might recruit children to study a mentor text written by a published author and help them notice that the text incorporates a sidebar, some captions, and a diagram. As children notice some of the special features in the text, push their thinking by saying to them, "Talk to your partner. Why do you think the writer might have used that?" and "Turn and tell you partner. What should we call this?" You might then use sticky notes to label these text features. Chances are that sidebars, captions, and diagrams are familiar to most of your students, so this will be a review—and a reminder to use all that they already know.

Bend I will probably end with children using the information checklist for second grade to notice what they are doing and not yet doing. Be sure you encourage children to look at the checklist for third grade also: the Common Core is not especially ambitious at these very early levels. It is best if you teach second-graders to be able to meet all the third-grade expectations for information writing. Your students won't all accomplish this goal, but if you teach toward it, you are giving those who need additional time the opportunity for the extended practice they need.

By this point in the unit, you will certainly have studied student work to help you plan instruction for the upcoming portion of the unit. When you review student work, look first at the organizational structure. Some children will find this a struggle. If many of your students have created a hodgepodge of information, you might decide to linger in the first bend of the unit for a few more days before moving on. Once children have a sense of organization, you'll want to teach them to elaborate—to teach more information in each chapter and to draw on a repertoire of strategies for making their writing interesting as well as informative.

BEND II: WRITE WITH ELABORATION: STUDY A MENTOR TEXT TO MAKE INFORMATION BOOKS LONGER AND MORE INTERESTING

Teach writers to generate and answer questions.

To start this bend, you might teach a minilesson that gives kids a sense of the big goal you have in mind: that their information books can be longer and more interesting. You might teach kids that *readers* of information texts ask themselves questions to make sure that they understand what they are reading: "Who is this about? Where are they? When is this happening? What are they doing? How are they doing it? Why are they doing it?" *Writers* can check each chapter to see that all those key questions have been answered, so that the reader isn't left wondering, "Huh? What's going on here?" In particular, thinking, "Why is this important?" sets children up to move beyond recording information to developing ideas. The Common Core emphasizes that information writers in second grade need to be able to generate and answer questions such as these.

When students write *where* something is, *how* something works, or *why* something is a particular way, often this results in more complex sentences and a more compelling book. Teach children how to expand their sentences using connector words (*so, and, but*), prepositional phrases (*in front of, behind, on top of*), and information language such as *most, some,* and *for example,* thus lending more clarity and precision to their writing. Then, too, you will want to help writers include transitional phrases to help guide readers.

Provide materials that give kids growing space.

If you've chosen a mentor text such as *Pandas* by Anne Schreiber or *Hamsters* by Bobbie Kalman, then you'll be able to show kids that information writers usually do not just write one sentence for each chapter and move on. Instead, they elaborate. They say more. You might start by giving your students the big picture, telling them that they should simply try to say more, just like the authors they read, and if they're going to write more, then they're going to need more lines, more pages.

As children begin incorporating more information into their chapters, those chapters won't fit on a single page. You'll want to notice when your students need growing space and give them that space. I have found it can help to suggest that each chapter in an information book become a three-page booklet. For example, in a book titled "All about Sharks," one chapter might be "Sharks Need to Swim," and within that chapter there may be three pages—one about sharks swimming to catch prey, one about sharks swimming to travel, and one about sharks swimming so that water passes through their gills and delivers oxygen. When a writer plans a whole page for each of these facts, there is room to elaborate on each one instead of just listing everything on one page.

Write with examples, just like mentor authors.

With whole booklets instead of single pages for chapters, kids have a visual prompt that signals to them that there is room to say more about each fact. They have more room now to try out all of the strategies that they might find contained in their mentor text. One strategy for elaboration is to use examples. In *Hamsters*, Bobbie Kalman writes one chapter that gives many examples of different kinds of hamsters. You might say to your kids, "She didn't just write, 'There are lots of kinds of hamsters,' and turn the page to start a new chapter. No! She gave examples! You can do that too!" If in a book titled "Video Games" a child writes, "There are a lot of different driving games," she could then give a lot of examples by saying, "For example, Mario Karts is a driving game. Another example is Diddy Kong." Then, of course, a student might elaborate on each example by describing or defining each example or item. You might teach kids to remember that sometimes they may be writing about things that other kids or adults have never heard of. They have to reread their own writing often to think, "What if I didn't know anything about this?" and then add descriptions and definitions to help the reader along.

Help students know the value of specific, detailed factual evidence that supports whatever they have written. For example, the author Anne Scheiber, in *Pandas*, uses many lists and specific details and measurements to say more about her information. Your kids can do that too! If a child writes, "We learn a lot of stuff in writing workshop," that child needs to include specific information about what he learns in writing workshop. Perhaps he'll tell about the different kinds of writing he does or perhaps he'll detail some strategies he has learned for writing more powerful pieces. Writing partners can help each other do this by asking questions and prompting each other, saying: "Say more." "What do you mean?" "Give an example."

Kids can also be taught to use quotations, numbers, and specific examples. If a writer has written, "Dogs eat a lot," the text is infinitely more effective if he follows this with, "For example, we went through three small bags of dog food in just one week."

Introduce students to the power—and risks—of research.

For the most part, kids will use facts and information that they already know, but you'll also want to introduce a very simple research strategy or two for finding specific quotations, numbers, and examples. For now, you might teach children that they can ask a partner for information, or you may teach them how to use a kid-friendly search engine on a classroom or technology lab computer to find information.

Whether they find the information they need from a friend or a website, you can teach kids that information writers always say where the information came from—they cite their sources. For now, you might teach kids a few simple prompts for citing sources, such as, "According to my friend Sarah, her cat eats twice a day, at nine o'clock and at five o'clock," or "The website National Geographic Little Kids taught me that there are about five thousand different kinds of ladybugs in the world."

Support elaboration.

Of course, some students will take your lesson on citing specific quotations, numbers, and examples to heart, and before you know it you'll begin to see booklets filled with lists of fact upon fact. Explain to children that citing and discussing evidence is almost like having a partnership conversation, only instead of talking to a person, they are talking to the page. When you teach someone information, it would be confusing and overwhelming if you simply listed tons and tons of facts. Instead when you are writing to teach others, it helps if you not only list the facts but also think about the facts and put that thinking in writing on the page. You can teach your students a few scaffolds for such thinking-on-the-page by giving them a list of thought prompts: "This is important because . . . " "You might be surprised to learn that . . . " "This shows that . . . " "I used to think . . . but now I know . . . " "The thing I am realizing about this is . . . " "The surprising thing about this is . . . " "Notice that . . . "

There are many reasons that writers elaborate on portions of text to say more. One purpose is setting up a reader to envision. For example, writers of all-about books show rather than tell in much the same way that fiction writers do. Information writers help readers picture what is happening, including how something looks or feels. A child writing "All about Scooters" might write, "Scooters can go really fast. Imagine you are going really fast on a scooter. You can feel the wind on your face!" Information writers can also use comparisons to help readers picture things. In a book about gymnastics, a child might write, "A cartwheel is a fun, easy trick to do in gymnastics. A cartwheel is like making your body into a pinwheel. You spin upside down and right side up." Or in a book about butterflies, "A butterfly uses its proboscis to suck the nectar out of a flower. The proboscis is like a straw. It's like the butterfly is sipping nectar out with a straw!"

Teach students strategies for how to introduce the topic as well as conclude with a final thought.

As you near the end of the second bend of this unit, your kids will now have a number of booklets collected in their writing folders. Now is a perfect time to teach students to introduce (not just name) a topic and to provide a concluding statement or section at the end (not just provide a sense of closure). It is wise that you have waited to teach this part of information text structure. Writers often get stymied when they draft introductions before drafting the main sections of a book. The introduction forecasts how the book will go, and often kids feel they cannot make changes if they have already drafted an introduction that suggests the book will go a certain way. Teaching introductions and conclusions simultaneously allows you to point out the similarities between these sections and gives kids a platform for sharing the ideas they have generated about the information as they wrote and revised chapters.

You might begin by examining your mentor texts together with your kids. For example, if you've selected a mentor text like *Pandas* by Anne Schreiber, you might teach children that they too can write an introduction that speaks directly to the readers to grab their attention and spark interest in the topic. In a minilesson you might say, "Let's take a look at Anne Schrieber's introduction." Then you'll read the first paragraph, highlighting the moves she has made as a writer. "'Look! Up in the tree! Is it a raccoon? No! It's a *Giant Panda!*'" Together, you and the students might discuss the way the author used short sentences or how she used a variety of punctuation and bold words. Perhaps you'll highlight how she used a question in the introduction or how she is talking directly to the reader. All of these are strategies that your students might try out in their own information books.

Many teachers find that writing an introduction in which the writer works to rally interest among readers generates interest and investment in the topic in the *writer*, too. In a minilesson, for example, you might tell the story of when you first became interested in your topic and what kindled that interest. Then demonstrate writing that story as an introduction for your piece of writing. In a book about cooking, for example, you might say, "I fell in love with cooking the first time I made chocolate chip cookies with my mom. I still remember how proud I was. Read this book to fall in love with cooking just like I did!"

Then again, a writer might address the reader directly: "Have you ever stopped to think about . . . Every time you do . . . you are . . . " "Did you know that . . . " Then, having provoked readers' interest, this writing might launch into an overview of the topic to introduce the book. For example, if the book teaches readers about NASCAR racing, the introduction could quickly preview what the chapters will be. "Have you ever been to a NASCAR race? In this book you will learn all about NASCAR. You'll learn about various race car drivers, the kinds of cars they drive, and the most important races."

Once you have taught students one or two strategies for writing introductions, you might encourage them to go back to *all* the books they have written so far and create introductions. Once they've revised all their old writing using everything they now know, they can write new books, using introductions from now on (though they can always write the whole book first and the introduction last). There are lots of other ways that the introduction can be written, and you'll want to share examples of especially well-crafted ones that you or your kids come up with. You may want to encourage kids to try alternative drafts of their introductions by saying them out loud several times to themselves or their writing partner. It will help, too, that because your writers have various book topics and titles, they can try out different sorts of introductions in different books.

Next you would turn to conclusions. Teach your second-graders that their concluding section is their final opportunity to get readers to care about the information they are teaching. The writer gets the last word. This is the perfect section for writers to share some of the ideas and opinions they have been developing about their topics. You might also teach writers that they should revisit or summarize some of the most important information from the text so that readers remember the main points. The main thing is that they understand that an information text doesn't just end. There is a final thought, and it's often the thing that their readers will remember most, since it is the last page they will read in the book.

Help students keep their engagement level high and their writing thoughtful.

Even with children reaching for more to say in each section of their writing, you'll want to be sure to keep up a high level of engagement and volume. The goal is to encourage students to try out new strategies for elaboration and specificity but not to bog kids down to a point where they are stumped and aren't sure what else to write. Also, watch out for students who have spent so long with a topic that their level of engagement seems to be dwindling. For example, after four days, you can expect the children to have written at least four multipage chapters, and even those they have revised extensively will not be perfect. The writing they have done will likely leave lots of room for improvement. That is to say, make sure your students are writing as best they can *and moving on*—to another page, another chapter, another book.

Children should be writing at a fluent pace, trying to get down as much as possible onto the page, generating more and more thinking. You may want to coach students along, reminding them that soon there will be plenty of time for researching and revising just one topic. Now is the time to continue collecting booklets on as many different topics as possible. So, while the emphasis in this bend in the road is on elaboration and specificity, you'll want to be careful that students don't feel stumped, that they do the best they can and move on.

At this point in the unit you may decide to hold a writing celebration. We suggest you keep it low key and intimate, because the end-of-unit celebration will be more significant. Options for this celebration include having students choose one book to share with a partner or a small group or perhaps setting up an expert museum, where students display their chosen book on their desk and then wander through the classroom, reading the books written by their peers. You may even decide to leave feedback sheets next to each book, so students can respond to what they have read. You can coach students to leave effective feedback for one another. Encourage them to say more than "I like your writing." Show them that it is a lot more helpful for writers to hear exactly what they did well—so that they can do it again the next time they write. Perhaps you'll show kids how they can use the charts around the room as a source of ideas for what to compliment in each other's writing. "We've got all these great strategy charts," you'll remind kids. "As you read each other's writing, you might notice where others have been trying out all the strategies from our unit. When you notice that a classmate has tried one of these strategies, you could write a note on their feedback sheet saying, 'I notice that you . . .'" These compliments will be far more instructional and helpful to your children as writers than generic comments that say, "You have neat handwriting," or "I like your drawings."

BEND III: REVISE ONE BOOK AND CONDUCT RESEARCH TO CREATE AN EXPERT PROJECT

Narrow the focus: guide students to choose one topic to explore in depth to create an expert project.

This bend marks the beginning of a very exciting writing project for your young writers. Think of a time in your own life when you have had the chance to dive deep into a topic that you had great interest in. Perhaps you've experienced the obsession of researching dog breeds in anticipation of getting a new puppy, or maybe you spent an entire summer reading nothing but parenting books to prepare for the arrival of a new baby in the family. Or perhaps you've been a lifelong history buff or avid reader of technology blogs and magazines. Maybe you like to blog or are a Pinterest fan. Adults and children alike feel a sense of satisfaction exploring a topic of interest. At the start of this bend, children will look over all the books they have drafted so far and choose one to turn into an expert project. They will then research and write about this project for the remainder of the unit.

To help children choose their expert projects, you will want to encourage them to choose a topic on which they have more to say—as well as one that they can easily research (by collecting information from books and especially by making observations). Ideally they will choose a topic that they've already written a book on, though in a few cases it might be wise to start with a fresh topic. Let kids know they will either be adding many more chapters to the book they've already begun to write or that they will be writing a whole collection of books on this topic. The choice can be theirs, or you may decide to steer your class one way or another. You might even show kids a few mentor texts that exemplify an expert project. For example, the *National Geographic Readers* series (by various authors) on transportation (*Trucks, Planes, Trains*) might as a whole be a mentor expert project. They also have a series on animals (*Penguins, Pandas, Sea Turtles*). In a minilesson, you might tell your students about a time you became obsessed with a topic and teach your kids that often writers have a topic that they love so much they can't possibly just write one book or a few chapters about it. They have so much to teach!

At first students will study their writing, using what they already know about the topic to be sure they have enough information and that their writing is clear to readers. Now is the ideal time to introduce a checklist that lets kids know your biggest priorities and goals for the unit. The checklist might contain just a few items, selected from the information writing checklist from grade 2 (or perhaps grades 2 and 3). The Information Writing Checklist, Grades 2 and 3 can be found on the CD-ROM.

1. In the beginning, I named a subject and tried to interest readers.

2. My writing has different parts. Each part tells different information about the topic.

3. I wrote a sentence or section at the end to wrap up my piece.

4. I used different kinds of information in my writing, such as facts, steps, and tips.

5. I tried to include the words that show that I'm an expert on the subject.

Children may look over their chapters and realize they need to revise headings, rewrite particular chapters, rearrange sections to support their readers, or even start another book on the topic to begin a collection of books. Students may also work with a partner to lift the level of their writing and help each other find places where they need to add more information or say more inside a particular chapter. You might teach students to listen to their partner's work with a specific lens in mind. Does each chapter have enough information? Do some chapters have too much information and others not enough? Do some chapters not fit with the selected structure? How could they be rewritten so that they do fit?

Teach students how to collect resources and conduct research (make close observations).

Encourage writers to consider what sorts of resources they could consult to research their topics. Even if they already know a lot about something, there is always more to learn. Research needn't mean only consulting books. If a child considers writing about fish that are excellent swimmers, she might gather information by observing her own fish as it swims in the tank or by visiting a pet store. Engaging in research about a topic that children know well gives them practice gathering information about a topic (CCSS W.2.8) before they delve into researching unknown topics. In some cases your children will have chosen topics about which information and ideas are easily available. A child who is writing about trees, for example, can easily look out the classroom window and make an observation. Likewise, a child who is writing about the class pet can pull his chair over to the guinea pig cage.

Now that your kids have chosen their topics and begun work, you might help spark their engagement and interest by inviting them to bring in resources from home to assist with their research. Ideally the majority of your students will have chosen topics that hold deep personal significance, and therefore they will be likely to have some resources at home that are relevant to the topic they chose. You may want to send a note home inviting parents and caregivers to help their child put together a few artifacts and resources relating to their topic—photographs, small relevant toys, clippings from magazines or online resources, books. Sending home a gallon-size ziplock bag or a shoebox in which to collect the resources will help kids gather material of the appropriate amount and size. Of course, you will scour your classroom (and your colleagues' rooms) and the school library for anything you can find to support the topics your students are researching. Not to worry—just a few small objects or a few nice photographs clipped from a magazine are all each kid really needs, at a minimum, to practice some of the research skills you'll be teaching next. You need not purchase an entire text set for every topic (though having a few related books never hurts).

When kids bring their resource collections to school, there is bound to be a wonderful conversation about the wide variety of objects, texts, and pictures. A child researching dogs may fill his box with a leash,

Information Writing Checklist

	Grade 2	NOT YET	STARTING TO	YES!	Grade 3	NOT YET	STARTING TO	YES!
	Structure				**Structure**			
Overall	I taught readers some important points about a subject.	☐	☐	☐	I taught readers information about a subject. I put in ideas, observations, and questions.	☐	☐	☐
Lead	I wrote a beginning in which I named a subject and tried to interest readers.	☐	☐	☐	I wrote a beginning in which I got readers ready to learn a lot of information about the subject.	☐	☐	☐
Transitions	I used words such as *and* and *also* to show I had more to say.	☐	☐	☐	I used words to show sequence such as *before*, *after*, *then*, and *later*. I also used words to show what didn't fit such as *however* and *but*.	☐	☐	☐
Ending	I wrote some sentences or a section at the end to wrap up my piece.	☐	☐	☐	I wrote an ending that drew conclusions, asked questions, or suggested ways readers might respond.	☐	☐	☐
Organization	My writing had different parts. Each part told different information about the topic.	☐	☐	☐	I grouped my information into parts. Each part was mostly about one thing that connected to my big topic.	☐	☐	☐
	Development				**Development**			
Elaboration	I used different kinds of information in my writing such as facts, definitions, details, steps, and tips.	☐	☐	☐	I wrote facts, definitions, details, and observations about my topic and explained some of them.	☐	☐	☐
Craft	I tried to include the words that showed I'm an expert on the topic.	☐	☐	☐	I chose expert words to teach readers a lot about the subject. I taught information in a way to interest readers. I may have used drawings, captions, or diagrams.	☐	☐	☐

a collar, a bone, and a brush. Another child might bring in a bird's nest found in the backyard and her mom's bird identification book. Highlight that even grown-up researchers use a wide range of sources to find information. Take some time to allow students to share their collections with their writing partners and talk all about what they are now planning to add to their expert project.

With this wide range of resources at your students' fingertips during writing workshop, you might decide to teach first how to make close observations of pictures, photos, and objects, since each of their collections will include something of that nature. If an artifact doesn't fit into an existing chapter, the child can write about it on a separate page titled, aptly, "Artifact" and then find a place for this new information later. Or he may create a new chapter (or a new book to add to a collection of books) if the artifact feels important enough to stand on its own.

Teach kids that researchers look at the entire picture or object, all the way from the top to the bottom, from left to right. They draw it in detail, trying not to miss anything, all the while thinking about key information questions: "What is this? What does it do? How does it do it? Why?" As they observe and draw, they think about the words they will use to describe the artifact, and then they write as much as they can about what they observed and what they are thinking about it. You might teach a few prompts ("I notice . . . ," "I see . . . ," "This reminds me of . . .") that help students elaborate on their observations. One way to ensure that the children are doing this writing in as much detail as possible is to teach them to observe with categories like color, texture, shape, and size in mind. If a child who has brought in a few of her cat's favorite toys describes all that she sees in great detail, this will make her book about cats more interesting and informative. You can even show students how they can use specific tools to help write and collect information. Students can use rulers to jot specific measurements, graph paper to draw true to scale, and hand lenses to see every little detail.

Many students will have brought in books related to their topics, and you will have added books you found that relate to their topics. Many of these books will contain photos, captions, and sections that your students can study. You might designate a few minutes of class time for kids to browse the books in their collections. Teach students that when writers include information from a book, they always cite their source, so that the readers can go back to the source and read this for themselves. You might teach students that when they want to use information from a book, they can look in the book to remember the information, then *close the book* and write what they know. You might say, "If you forget what the book taught you, that's a good sign that you need to reread more carefully, so that you really know the information well."

Put the research to use. Teach children a variety of formats.

Some of the artifacts, texts, and other resources are likely to remind children of experiences that they have had that relate to their expert project topic. They might want to write a Small Moment chapter about such an experience, describing the moment bit by bit, in sequence. You might show students examples of narrative writing (stories) that incorporate information that teaches about the topic—the book *Pumpkins* by Ken Robbins, for example, or the narrative sections of some of Gail Gibbons's books. In a minilesson, you might show children that to write a Small Moment chapter, they can use all the strategies they know about great stories: stretch the story details across the pages using dialogue, thoughts, and actions, just as they would when writing any story.

Then too, the artifacts will trigger a variety of new chapters. A dog's leash can result in a diagram of the different parts of the leash, with several sentences about each of the parts and their purposes. A set of toys from a popular game (Angry Birds or Bey Blades, for example) might be the inspiration for a how-to chapter ("How to Play Bey Blades" or "How to Win at Angry Birds"). In fact, many of your students will be working on projects that lend themselves to a how-to chapter or booklet. Of course, you'll want to remind students of some pointers for writing strong procedural writing: acting the steps out with a partner, for example, can help the writer plan what to write. Saying each step, bit by bit, in very clear precise words also helps one write a strong how-to. Using transitional words (*first*, *then*, *next*) helps the reader keep track of the steps, and speaking directly to the reader in the imperative *you* (instead of the first-person *I*) also makes the directions easier to follow. Some how-to books and manuals include a materials page. Others include cautions or warnings for the reader. Encourage kids, as always, to say their writing aloud a few times before writing it to clarify what they really want to say.

As your students work, they should be able to incorporate a range of academic and domain-specific words—the lingo of the particular topic's field—into their writing. In conferences you might explicitly teach a few key words to help children write with more clarity and use more sophisticated words. You might ask a student to point to all the parts of a picture or a diagram he has created and supply some key vocabulary words where they are needed. You might also support kids' acquisition of new vocabulary by choosing to read aloud books that connect with the children's topics, so that kids writing about animals or sports or whatever the topics happen to be are hearing (and using) lots of animal or sports or other topic-related vocabulary during the read-alouds. Encourage children to use new words when they talk and when they write, even when they are not entirely sure they are using the new terminology well. Approximation is the first step to learning.

Remind students of what they know about writing strong introductions and conclusions.

As you move children through the process of drafting and revision, you'll certainly want to spend some time revisiting the art of writing introductions and conclusions, referring back to what they learned earlier in the unit. Along the way, some of your children will realize that they can and should revise or remove their original introductions and conclusions as they add new chapters, revise, and remove sections of their work. You might find a few examples of this revision work to share with your class and suggest that your kids repeatedly reread their entire expert project to make sure all the parts, including the introduction and conclusion, still make sense. In conferences you might teach a few children to write stronger conclusions and then share those with the whole class in a mid-workshop teaching point or a share at the end of the workshop.

As children begin to declare their books done, be sure that you can see signs of their revision work. A complete piece may have sentences crossed out, flaps added to make room for more writing, labels added to diagrams, headings written and rewritten, some chapters added, and others removed. Teach children to reread and fix up their work to make sure it all makes sense, too, crossing out parts that "don't go" and fixing parts that are confusing. Children might need to rework chapters (starting fresh sometimes) to draw out the main idea they are trying to show. Partners often help each other write with more precision or decide whether they need more information or ideas in their chapters. Partners can also teach a chapter of their books to each other, checking for clarity and gaps that need to be filled. Children should review their tables of contents, too, to be sure these reflect their final chapter selection, and decide whether they want to add a glossary of terms.

BEND IV: EDIT, FANCY UP, AND PUBLISH THE WRITING SO THAT IT TEACHES IN CLEAR AND EXCITING WAYS

Plan your celebration—the preliminaries.

You have taught children to consider their audience throughout this unit, and now you might invite them to think carefully about who they would like to invite to the celebration—who might stand to learn from their particular topics. At the start of this bend, children could write letters or invitations or even posters to announce their celebration to individuals or to a group—perhaps another classroom or the administration of your school or a younger group of children. Of course, you will want to check a few weeks in advance to be sure that the other class, administrators, or younger group is able to come to the celebration.

This unit lends itself well to having an expert fair—akin to a science fair but with the full range of topics that your students have chosen to research. Children can teach others what they know about their topics. Every celebration you do in your classroom is an opportunity to work on presentation skills—to teach strategies for speaking, such as pointing to pictures and visual aids as one speaks. Likewise, you might teach strategies for listening—as simple as taking turns but also restating what your partner just taught you and asking questions for clarification. Yes, you want the event to feel celebratory, but you also want kids to know this is important, challenging work.

Teach students the importance of making their writing easy to read.

With the celebration fast approaching, your students have a real reason to make sure that their work is easy for others to read—that they have used their best spelling, handwriting, and punctuation. Chances are, you have been encouraging your children to check that they spell word wall words correctly and draw on spelling patterns also as they write. Use mid-workshop teaching points to remind students to use all that they know to write as conventionally as possible. Don't hesitate to emphasize that it's important to use capital and lowercase letters appropriately, as well as ending punctuation and quotation marks. A helpful chart could list editing non-negotiables, such as capital letters, ending punctuation, and word wall words, and you might remind your students to refer to the editing chart often to proofread their work on a routine basis.

You may want to teach children to reread their books with an eye toward writing more complex sentences, stopping after each sentence and thinking, "Is this the best way to say this? Do I like the way this sounds?" You might then teach them how to rearrange the wording or combine two sentences to write compound sentences with clauses and more sophisticated punctuation. Help your students understand that this is what editing work is really all about—moving words around, playing with language, and trying out different options to make sure everything sounds right and looks right. They need not depend completely on you to tell them each and every specific thing to edit. They should always be thinking, "Does this look right? Does this sound right?" And, along with using all the editing charts and lessons you have provided, they should problem solve ways to make their writing easy for others to read and understand.

Near the end of this unit, you might introduce a few new editing strategies to add to their growing repertoire, such as using commas to separate the elements in a list, capitalizing proper nouns, and indenting each new paragraph. The booklets your students have been creating are well set up for paragraphing. Each new page in a chapter is ready-made to be organized around a central idea, so it is not a big stretch to teach students to indent at the start of each new idea—at the top of a new page. As the year goes on, you may even begin to see some students writing on lined paper and organizing their thoughts into paragraphs simply by pretending there are separate pages on the lined paper and indenting for each new one—and voila! Paragraphs!

Fancy up writing for publication by highlighting text features and rehearsing for presentations.

Now is also the time to let kids know that guests will soon be reading their work, and just as people like to clean up their house when guests come over, writers like to "fancy up" their writing for their readers. There are many meaningful ways kids can fancy up their writing so that they are working for a purpose higher than simply decorating. Some people think that underlining, bolding, or putting a box around important vocabulary helps the reader figure out which words are important to the topic. Writers may also define the terms in a simple glossary. Now is the time to make sure that the page numbers on the table of contents are correct and that the headings for each chapter are capitalized appropriately and match the chapter titles listed in the table of contents. This work has the added benefit of helping your children recognize and use these nonfiction features in the books they read and will also give them a sense of being real authors.

As your writers get their pages ready to share with an audience, they might make front and back covers for their books. Your young writers will love writing back-cover blurbs that persuade readers to choose their book: "Read this book if you want to be an expert at soccer!" "Sharks can be our friends! Famous author Carly Smith explains the truth about sharks." To support kids in this work, you might create a chart of words that often appear on the backs of nonfiction books, such as *surprising, famous, exciting, thrilling, find out, explore*. This will encourage kids to think carefully about word choice. Then, on to the front cover. Your writers can probably do more than write the title. They can think carefully about the colors and the picture they will put on the cover and how those will influence the reader—just as the front covers of books they pick up influence them. Kids who have chosen their own cover images carefully study the covers of non-fiction more carefully. However you decide to wrap up the unit, be sure to design your last lessons to help students to prepare for publishing their work while making the best use of every last minute of the unit.

To prepare for the expert fair, you might use one last writing workshop to teach children to rehearse a mini-presentation. Explain to your students that they are such great experts on their topics and have so much to say that they couldn't possibly squeeze it all into the short time available for the expert fair. Instead, they might prepare to tell visitors the most important things about their topics, most likely by giving a brief introduction and an overview of their chapter titles and some key information. As visitors enter the classroom, they'll be invited to stand by individual students and listen to their presentations. Then they might circulate around the room, so that students have several opportunities to present.

Celebrate!

The expert fair could take place on a small scale, with students simply talking about and pointing to pictures in the books they have written as various visitors step up to their desk or table. Alternatively, this could become a larger project involving some outside preparation at home or during another part of the day. Perhaps you'll coordinate with the technology or library media specialists in your building so that kids might create simple PowerPoint or Keynote presentations about their books. Alternatively, students might make presentation boards on which to display their expert project books and use a pointer to present their work. A child who wrote a book about scooters might set up a presentation board with photographs of herself riding her scooter, complete with captions, her "All about Scooters" book proudly displayed at the center. She might even bring in her scooter, helmet, and knee pads. Then, as she presents, she might give a brief demonstration of how to ride. Use your imagination and make plans for a celebration that matches the interests of the audience, the resources available, and the needs of your students.

During the expert fair and afterward, you will want to display *all* your children's work, complete with extensive revisions. On a bulletin board, you might use sticky notes to proudly label some of the revision work your students tried out. "I tried comparisons!" a sticky note might say, with an arrow pointing to the exact place where the student did the work. No matter how you decide to celebrate the work your students have done, you'll want to give them a chance to reflect on the work of the unit, perhaps by talking with a partner about what they learned or using a checklist to record all the unit goals they have successfully met. You might provide kids with an example of an informational book that meets all the goals of the unit, and then make a chart naming all the things the writer did. Then, ask your students to check through their own writing to see whether they did all the same things, to celebrate what they accomplished, and to set goals for the next time they will write informational books.

Writing Gripping Fictional Stories with Meaning and Significance

RATIONALE/INTRODUCTION

This unit has been a longtime favorite of young children. As any teacher of young students knows, children's imaginations are brimful of story ideas—and your class will be chomping at the bit to start putting theirs onto the page. They'll approach this unit with abundant ambition and zeal, ready to write, write, write. Chances are that children who eked out words during the previous unit will write with new volume, new stamina, and new engagement, their scrawl filling one page, then another and another as the unit taps into a great source of energy.

This genre of writing may or may not be new to your kids. Whether they have already experienced a unit in fiction writing or simply have a handful of personal narrative units under their belts, they can get a great deal out of this month. How you spin the unit—and what you teach—will depend largely on your particular students. Chances are, your kids know a thing or two about crafting Small Moment stories. They know that it helps to zoom in on a particular scene—say, an event that occurs across fifteen minutes—and to write the story of that event in a step-by-step fashion so that readers can relive the event, picturing what the main character said and did first and then what occurred in response. If children have experienced units of study on narrative writing, they'll also approach this unit already knowing about the value of stretching out the most important parts of those stories.

On the other hand, if children have not studied writing through units of study in K–1, they may not have been taught what we regard as a crucial concept: that it is far easier to write an effective story if one zooms in on a small moment, a particular scene, and writes that small moment, that scene, as a storyteller might tell it, allowing readers to almost live in the shoes of the character. That is, a child who has not studied Units of Study in Writing might approach the project of writing a story about a boy who learns to do a magic trick, planning to start the story, "Once upon a time a boy named Michael wanted to do a magic trick and so he did it. The audience cheered and he smiled big." Contrast that lead with, "Michael held his deck of cards. He walked up to the stage and said, 'Good evening, ladies and gentlemen.'" You'll need, then, to be sure to highlight this part of your instruction. The unit contains lots of spaces for you to do that.

Either way, children come to this unit with a background not only as writers but also as readers. They've read narrative picture books and chapter books in which each chapter is rather like a self-contained story. Your children's experiences with short stories (whether in picture books, in episodic chapter books, or in collections of short stories) provides them with a reservoir to draw upon. It will be important for them to understand that they are being asked to write in ways that re-create the sounds and rhythms of stories. As you help children draw on their knowledge as readers, keep in mind that you are supporting their abilities to talk and think about published texts and about the author's craft in those texts. This is highly supportive of CCSS reading standards 4, 5 and 6.

This unit prioritizes story structure, spotlighting the plotting work that a short story writer does, emphasizing especially that a good story contains a scene (or small moment) or two and is told to build gripping tension. The character wants something and encounters trouble en route to that something. For your children, you capture this combination of motivations and obstacles by characterizing the stories they'll be writing as "edge of the seat stories" or "trouble stories." That is, this is not just about a character who does something (performs a magic trick in front of an audience). It is about a character who wants something, who encounters trouble. The story comes not from performing the magic trick, but from wanting to do well and struggling to master the trick. Tension can turn a sequential chain of events into something that feels like a story. To do this, teach your students how to develop characters in a way that builds tension, giving them dreams, desires, fears, and frustrations.

One big goal of this unit (and any writing unit) is to increase the volume of writing your children produce. Meanwhile, you will also aim to raise the quality of your children's narrative writing. In this unit, then, you will remind children of what they already know about good narrative writing and then extend that repertoire, bearing in mind that the ultimate goal is for children to write well-elaborated short stories.

Before you begin this unit, think back to when you were about eight years old. Chances are, you recall a story or two you wrote or wanted to write. Was there a character in that story who had a giant feeling welling up inside of her or him? Did that character want something—a friend, a prize, a chance—so badly it hurt? These are the feelings your children have surely had, and their characters can have these feelings too. Teach kids that in good fiction, characters' wants, hopes, and aches are big. Then give your students space to write—and let their imaginations run free.

A SUMMARY OF THE BENDS IN THE ROAD FOR THIS UNIT

In the first bend (Think of a Character and of Small Moment Stories for That Character: Generating and Writing Several Short Fiction Books), you will set children up to generate edge of the seat story ideas and then quickly choose one, first storytelling it to a partner before sitting down to write, write, write. Children will write several focused stories during this first bend, writing in booklets. To do this they will draw both on everything they have learned about good narrative writing and on new strategies that you teach—on storytelling focused Small Moment scenes rather than summarizing, on using detail to build tension, and on stretching out the most gripping parts. Plan to spend at least a week in this bend. If children have never been in a Small Moment unit of study, this will require at least a week and a half.

In Bend II (Revise with Intention: Pull Readers to the Edges of Their Seats), children will return to the stories they have written, revising these stories for greater meaning and tension. They may revise by writing whole new versions of their stories, reaching toward the goal of storytelling rather than summarizing. If they have written their stories in a such a way that the drama unfolds on the pages, then their revision will mostly involve reworking their drafting booklets, revising like carpenters. They'll add pages and flaps and extenders to their booklets as they learn how to stretch out the "heart" of the story (the part that gets readers gripping their seats in anticipation), how to complicate the problem, and also to build tension also by having the character attempt first one thing, then another, then another to solve the problem before finding a way to resolve things. In short, children will learn how to revise with intention, just as they did earlier in the year during the *Lessons from the Masters* unit. Allow about a week to make your way through Bend II.

In Bend III (Repeat the Process and Accumulate Lessons Along the Way), children will repeat the process, this time focusing on doing all that they can do to make their stories even better. Children will self-assess at the start of and throughout this bend, setting goals for themselves based on the narrative checklist, on charts around the room, and on what they see in their writing. To support this push toward writing the best stories possible, you may teach them strategies to be sure that the parts of their story fit together or teach them to write more compelling endings, perhaps ones that convey a message to readers. Bend III could also take a week and a half. Expect students to produce at least three stories (two in each week, or more if this bend is longer than that).

GETTING READY
Gather Texts for Students

As with all units of study, you will want to select mentor texts to accompany your teaching so that you can provide your writers with examples. Some gripping picture books we recommend using throughout this unit are *Shortcut*, by Donald Crews; *Too Many Tamales*, by Gary Soto; *Koala Lou*, by Mem Fox; and *The Ghost-Eye Tree*, by Bill Martin. Or you might use parts of an early-reader chapter book from a series (Kate DiCamillo's Mercy Watson, James Howe's Pinky and Rex, Barbara Park's Junie B. Jones, or Suzy Kline's Horrible Harry are some possibilities). And remember that you have stories from your life that you can write with meaning, significance, and tension as a way to demonstrate for your children all that is possible. You can tailor these pieces of writing to demonstrate the skills your students need.

Use Additional Resources as Needed

You will also want to consult books on children's literature because any such book can teach you the language that fiction writers use to describe their craft, and that language can lift your teaching in this unit. Of course it is always important to draw on the work of the children in your classroom. Workshop teaching is most powerful when you respond and teach to your kids' successes and struggles. In the end, a good portion of your teaching will revolve around the responsive instruction you provide as you move kids along trajectories of skill development. You'll want to become accustomed to fine-tuning your teaching through an attentiveness to student work, because the work your students do is not just showing you what they can or can't do; it is also showing you what *you* can do.

Choose When and How Children Will Publish

Your students are likely to generate many pieces of writing during this unit. During the second and third bends, you will emphasize revision, and students will have the opportunity to deeply revise a book from the first bend and another book from the third bend. Those final stories can all be published in some fashion. For the publishing celebration, however, children will presumably need to choose just one of those stories to share; perhaps it will be one that builds the most tension or carries the most significance. Just as the gripping stories you read aloud to your class are meant to be discussed, so too are the gripping stories your students will write worthy of discussion. You may want to model your celebration after your whole-class read-aloud, giving students an opportunity to read their stories aloud and then giving listeners a chance to have a discussion. That, of course, would need to happen in small groups. You might do this with just your class or perhaps invite outsiders to participate in the celebration.

BEND I: THINK OF A CHARACTER AND OF SMALL MOMENT STORIES FOR THAT CHARACTER: GENERATING AND WRITING SEVERAL SHORT FICTION BOOKS

Introduce the genre.

Your students will undoubtedly be eager to write fiction, especially as they become more and more immersed in the fictional worlds of the characters they meet in books. Throughout this unit, the most important message you'll convey is this: writers use everything they know to make up their own stories. You'll tell your children, "Using everything you have learned about strong narrative writing, you can write realistic fiction stories about a character you dream up." That is, you will want to make it clear to your children that while they are embarking on a new unit, they will want to bring all that they have already learned to the effort of writing realistic fiction stories. You will encourage writers to draw on all the craft moves they learned from studying mentor authors and all the strategies they now hold in their repertoire for writing small moments. The Common Core State Standards call for second-graders to write sequenced narratives while providing a sense of closure, so you will want to help your writers think about the arc and language of their stories, about the passage of time, and about the need for a conclusion that brings the story together. The goal for this unit will be to write well-elaborated short stories.

You might begin this unit by asking children to recall what they already know about writing narratives. Produce charts from your prior narrative unit, and announce that the class will use and build on strategies. Perhaps you'll ask children to bring a favorite published narrative they wrote earlier in the year with them to the carpet and then you can ask them to share some things they did that made that piece particularly strong.

Of course, you'll also want to make the new unit seem brand-new and exciting. You might say something like, "Writers, you have an exciting opportunity ahead of you. You are going to write edge-of-the-seat *fiction* stories. That means that you'll write stories that keep your readers wanting more, ones that make them think, 'Oh no, how will this story end?' and 'Oh my goodness, I can't wait to turn the page.' Edge-of-the-seat fiction stories are exactly what you think they are: fiction stories that put readers, literally, on the edge of their seat!"

You might then read an example of a story that is fictional, but realistic, and keeps readers on the edge of their seat. As mentioned earlier, *Shortcut*, by Donald Crews; *The Ghost-Eye Tree*, by Bill Martin; *Koala Lou*, by Mem Fox; and *Too Many Tamales*, by Gary Soto are four great examples, and they represent a range of ways to build tension. Some teachers share tension-filled clips from movies, like the garbage incinerator scene from *Toy Story 3*; if you elect to do that, you can narrate and story-tell as the scene unfolds to show children how a writer builds tension.

Meanwhile teach students to generate focused story ideas, choosing between them.

While you introduce the genre, you'll also take the first day or two of the unit to teach children a few strategies to generate Small Moment fictional stories—fictional episodes—in which a character encounters trouble and somehow resolves it. Children will not need more than two strategies for generating gripping stories, but they will use these strategies often because they'll probably generate a handful of possible ideas, then choose and write one story, then they'll generate another handful of ideas and choose and write another story. Over the course of the unit, they will write four to eight stories, so they'll generate lots of story ideas.

Both of the strategies that we most suggest involve students thinking of a strong emotion, one that they feel sometimes and that characters in the books they read also sometimes feel. The writer might select jealousy, embarrassment, frustration, surprise, or hope. And both of the strategies involve the writer making up a character and thinking of Small Moments stories (or "one time when" stories) in which that character had one of those feelings. One strategy for generating fictional stories begins with young writers thinking of "one time when's" from books that they have read. A child might think, for example, of the awful embarrassment Pinky felt when he wet his pants during the spelling bee (in *Pinky and Rex and the Spelling Bee*). Then the job is to create a similar moment for a fictional character. Maybe the child who began by thinking about Pinky's embarrassing moment might make up a story in which a character trips on the stage during a piano recital or forgets her lines during the school play or misses the ball during tryouts for the softball team. Another child who began by thinking of how desperately Ramona wants to pull her rival Susan Kushner's long blonde curls—and the moment when she does—might imagine his or her character is jealous of someone and longs to bring that person down in some way. Imagine the tension-filled scene leading up to the character's realizing this dream! The idea is to create a fictional character, zoom in on a strong emotion, and then create a time when that fictional character experienced that strong emotion.

Children's literature is full of characters who ache and want and worry and fume, so it won't be hard for your students to find an emotion or a scenario they can latch onto as a template they can borrow to help them with the story of their own making. Suspenseful fiction is full of stories of characters wanting something out of reach, not fitting in, getting into trouble, embarrassing themselves, facing danger. Your children, too, can draw on these topics and spin them in their own unique way.

Another strategy for coming up with an idea for a fictional story involves starting with small moments from one's own life instead of from literature. These stories can then be fictionalized or told from a different perspective to bring out the tension. For example, perhaps a student thinks of a moment when she was lost in the grocery store. In reality, she was only apart from her family for a minute or so, but in a realistic fiction story, the character might be lost for an entire day and maybe not in a grocery store but on the city streets. Often students will find that telling realistic stories based on real life is a powerful way to show how an event really felt. Sometimes the actual facts don't convey the powerful emotions that surround the moments from life that really matter.

Whichever strategy you teach and your children use, be sure that generating a list of possible realistic fiction ideas takes children ten minutes, not the entire workshop time, and that they then pick one to start writing about. Some teachers suggest that children generate something like four story ideas, then write the first page of a few of those stories, and then choose one to write as a whole story, leaving the remaining first pages as books-in-waiting.

As children plan stories, steer them to write with focus, limiting their characters and scope, and to plan through storytelling and sketching.

Your goal in this unit is for students to write stories that are comprised of two small moments (or scenes) at most, so this means it is essential that you guide your kids to select story ideas that can happen in one or two twenty-minute stretches of time. Make sure that many of the stories you study as mentor texts during this unit also cover short periods of time (picture books or short chapter books tend to work best for this), so that children have models. Likewise, children should focus on maybe two or three realistic characters rather than a large cast, and the main character should be close in age to the writer. This will allow your children to get into the head of that character and to develop all the characters with some essential details rather than presenting them superficially one after another on the page.

One of the ways to channel children toward stories that are limited in scope and follow a clear arc is to continually remind them of all they know about Small Moment personal narrative writing. Make sure you remind them that instead of writing "watermelon stories" in which they tell all about their character's life or time at camp, they are writing about a single seed story. Ask, "If you are writing about a character who went shopping at the mall and got lost, will you start when the character walks into the mall? When the character's mother says, 'I'll be right back?' Or when?"

Take time at the start of the unit to help children practice telling their stories aloud, telling their stories across pages of a drafting booklet a few times, first to themselves and then to their writing partners or to you during a conference or to the whole class during shares. As students improve their stories with each verbal retelling, make sure they have a system for quickly jotting down their ideas. For instance, they can sketch a quick, tiny picture in the top corner of each page to help them remember their plans. After they have story-told and planned their stories in their drafting booklets (which should take fifteen minutes, not days!) they need to draft. They'll need five- to seven-page booklets in which to write, with each page of the booklet essentially functioning like one dot in the timeline of the event. Imagine that it should take children no more than a day and a half to write the whole story, front to finish. We have found that if children prolong this process for too long, the stories become disjointed.

Encourage volume in both the quantity of stories generated and the depth of individual stories.

If some children get going strong, they may ask if they can staple more pages onto their booklets. We suggest that instead of encouraging sprawling, long stories, you channel your children's fervor for fiction into writing one fictional story after another. This also means that you'll want to teach students that "when you're done, you've just begun." When a story is completed, it can be stored on one side of the writing folder, with unfinished stories on the other side of the folder. After completing one story, the writer can then go back to choose another idea from a list generated earlier, or make a new list of story ideas, and complete the process again. There should never be a reason to be completely stuck. If a story has become difficult, the writer can store it in their folder and work on something else. From time to time you might remind students to reread all the stories in their folder to see whether there is more they might add to them. Children love to tell a good story—the kind that gets a reaction. Take this energy and use it to stretch their volume of writing. Expect most children to write two or three stories per week. Some might write two or three stories during the entire unit, but these will be children who write several completely new drafts per week. Either way, you will expect the volume to continually increase.

At the start of this unit, writers should be working in five-page booklets. As the unit progresses you may want to push them to write more, perhaps introducing booklets of loose-leaf paper that resemble what your children will encounter in third grade. You might say, "Writers, over the past few days I have noticed you going through more booklets than ever before. You are filling your five-page booklets and then picking up another one and beginning the next story. I'm thinking that instead of moving on to the next story, you might want to try to stretch one story. Before, you used to write in five-page booklets that had a few lines on each page, but now I see that you are ready to stretch your writing over more pages with more lines. You will write just as much as before, but this time instead of writing a few different stories, you are going to go deeper into one story, adding more and stretching it out to show the importance of it."

44

Use writing partners to help students elaborate with focus.

We hope that when presented with the added space, children's eyes will light up and their hands will begin to move faster than ever before. However, sometimes, children meet the business of writing longer stories with groans and complaints. Not surprisingly, the single most powerful ingredient in children's enthusiasm is your enthusiasm and attitude. If you focus too much on volume, demanding that students write a minimum number of pages, it is likely that students will bend their heads faithfully to this task, creating minimum pages that will be just that: minimum. Instead, if you present the opportunity to write longer stories as a new freedom or even as a characteristic of more accomplished writers, your young writers are more likely to be so excited by the challenge to fill the space that they will begin to write as much as possible across those pages. You might show how, as a writer comes to know more about how to craft a story, she simply needs more space to tell the story with all the details that help the story come alive for the reader. One teacher we know used a well-loved picture book and wrote an alternative version with only half the text, saying that the author might have chosen to write her story this way. She presented this bare-bones version to students, who easily recognized that the shorter story had lost much of its significance and power compared with the original. The same effect might be achieved using your own model text or the story of a shared class experience.

The challenge, of course, will be to help students write more while staying within two short episodes. The Common Core State Standards call for students to "recount a well-elaborated event or short sequence of events" (W.2.3). You do not want your students to elongate their stories by including extraneous details or writing "bed to bed" stories (a story that begins when the main character wakes up in bed in the morning and ends when the character goes to bed at night). Rather, you will want to help them keep their focus on a short snippet of their characters' lives, zooming in to elaborate with details that add tension. Help students stretch out the action in their episodes, going bit by bit through each small moment. For example, instead of writing, "I opened the door," a child might write, "I gripped the knob and pulled with all my might."

One strategy for helping students figure out how to say more is to encourage them to share their story with their writing partner, and to check whether their story is having the effect they hoped for. A writer might read the first portion of his story aloud and then ask, "What are you picturing?" or "Does that part make sense?" Feedback such as, "I'm confused. Can you say more?" or "What do you really mean?" can help writers to add more and more to their stories to clarify and extend. Their pages will become filled, and the need for more lines and extra pages will become clear. To practice visualizing how each bit of the story went, partners could act out their stories for each other. They can go page by page, acting out what happened, and then quickly writing down all the things they did. So the writer working on stretching out the part where he opens the door might stand up and act out opening a door with his partner. Then, the two can sit down and write all the little things that the writer had to do to get that door open.

BEND II: REVISE WITH INTENTION: PULL READERS TO THE EDGES OF THEIR SEATS

Teach students to make their stories come alive through storytelling with detail and thinking about the internal journey of their characters.

In this bend in the road of the unit, the focus shifts from drafting to revision, from writing with volume to writing effective stories. Your goal now is to dramatically improve your students' writing so that their stories come alive and brim with meaning. Toward this end, one important focus will be storytelling with detail, not summarizing. Teach children that to tell a story, a writer first decides what the story is about: "This is a story about a girl who wants a dog because all her friends have one. At first her parents say no, but eventually, after a struggle, she gets it." Next, the writer envisions each small moment of the story, rather than storytelling the whole of the story, which often leads children to summarize ("Emily wanted a dog. 'Can I have one?' she asked. Her mother said, 'No,' because they didn't have the money. Then one day she was walking to school and she saw something and it was a dog. The end.")

Teach children to ask themselves, "What, exactly, will happen at the start of my story?" The writer of the story about a girl who longs for a dog might think, "If the girl wants a dog, what can I have her do that shows this? If this were a play, what would she be doing on stage?" Perhaps the main character talks to her mother about getting a dog. The child might write, "Emily walked into the kitchen. Her mom was making dinner. 'Mom! Mom! Can I have a dog? Annie has one and it's really cute,' Emily whined." Or the writer might create an opening moment in which Emily gazes longingly at her friend's dog. Finally, teach children to make movies in their minds of the exact story, imagining it bit by bit, as they write.

Reliving stories, imagining the events unfolding, elicits writing that is organized and fluid. Children write sequenced stories with greater elaboration. One of the best ways to help children imagine a story is by acting it out. As children act out one moment, then another, they can not only record what each character says and does but also describe each bit of the story in detail, including where the characters are and what is happening around them. Partners can work together to find words that describe the actions and bring voice to the dialogue they act out together. Children can also look closely at the books they are reading to explore how these authors bring their favorite characters to life. Teach them how to study these texts to discover ways authors use time transitions to make each scene of their story flow. This will help children transition more smoothly from one part of the story to the next and also use more sophisticated sentence structures as they compose their own stories.

As your students story-tell and act out parts of their stories, they'll then turn to their drafts and make changes so that their written work matches their oral rehearsal. In the first bend you taught children that they could story-tell across the pages to figure out how the story might go and then make a quick sketch at the top of each page. In this bend, you might build on that strategy, teaching kids that they can sketch to plan what happens but also to plan how the character will feel on each page of the story. They can do this by either jotting a word or two along with the sketch or matching the faces of the characters to the feelings conveyed. You can share with kids that one of the many secrets to good fiction writing is that writers

46

pay attention to what's happening both on the outside of the character, and the inside. On the outside, a character might be walking down the street, carrying a backpack. On the inside, he's thinking, "I'm so nervous! I hope the other kids will like me!" As kids develop plans for new stories, they can begin to think about the internal journey of their characters (their thoughts, feelings, worries, struggles), as well as the external journey.

Children might also look to their favorite books and characters to see how good writers flesh out their characters in ways that bring them to life, showing their feelings rather than telling them. You might say, "To write stories that will draw readers in, you can look at the work of other writers who have done this, noticing how they show to bring their characters to life." "Emily walked into the kitchen where her mother stood cooking dinner. She said, 'Mom, I'm the only kid at school without a dog!' Emily had her fingers crossed." Notice how this example weaves dialogue with characters' actions. Teach your children to do likewise. Similarly, remind children that when they revise fiction, they can draw on the exact same techniques they used for revision of personal narratives. Keep your charts that support elaboration and revision from the previous unit front and center.

Create tension: include obstacles, complicating problems, and challenging situations.

Another important focus of this bend, of course, will be on building tension. Reiterate to your students that tension is that quality in a story that compels the reader to keep turning the pages out of eagerness to know what happens next. Tension keeps the reader on the edge of his seat! Writers weave tension throughout the story, especially at the beginning. Tension builds the momentum of the story. Early in a story, it can help to include a line or two that shows how the character is feeling or what she is thinking. This shows the inner story and piques readers' curiosity, encouraging them to read on, anticipating what will happen next. You might say to children, "You know how when you read, you often think, 'I bet such-and-such will happen next!' You want the readers of your stories to think like that too, but they need your help. They need you to drop a hint here or there so that they can begin to guess what might happen next. You can do this by sharing what a character is thinking or feeling."

The easiest way to create tension is to make it hard for the main character to get what he or she wants. In a story about a girl who wants desperately to visit her grandmother in South America, the writer should create a situation that keeps her from getting on that plane! The writer might ask herself, "What will make this difficult to achieve? Does the girl's father not want her to go? Is the girl afraid of flying? Is the plane ticket too expensive?" Encourage your writers to ask, "What trouble will get in my character's way, stop him from getting what he wants?"

Extra paper can also help with tension. Teach young writers to insert extra pages into the important parts of their stories to make sure they are telling those parts bit by bit, drawing them out. You are keeping them from just adding more pages at the end. This is revision with a purpose, as opposed to revision merely for the sake of revision.

Teach writers that as the story continues, they can add more hurdles that make things hard for the main character, and that leave the reader thinking, "What is going to happen next?!" You might teach kids that often there are several "bumps in the road." If you are modeling a story about the time two friends went bike riding and one had an accident, you might begin with the moment when one friend falls off her bike. Then, in the next part of your story, perhaps the other character notices that her friend has cut her upper lip and is bleeding. She tries to help her up to walk back home when she realizes that her friend has sprained her ankle and can't move. Now the problem spirals from a fall off the bike into a major accident, leaving the reader thinking, "Oh no! How are they going to get out of this?"

BEND III: REPEAT THE PROCESS AND ACCUMULATE LESSONS ALONG THE WAY

Reflect on past work and set goals for future work.

You can help children self-assess using the checklist for narrative writing. They can evaluate their writing, deciding whether it includes the skills on the learning progression, and if not, decide what they need to do to make sure that it does. You may also ask them to look for evidence of one or two additional skills that you have taught.

These concepts are sophisticated for young writers, so you will want children to practice them in lots of pieces. Each time they begin a new five-page booklet, encourage them to draw on all that they have learned so far, aiming to make their next book even better. You might say to children that the first thing any writer must do before beginning a new story is to sit down and think about what she knows makes for good writing. Then the writer sets a plan for what she will do to improve her writing. When writers embark on new stories, they need to ask themselves, "What did I do in my last story that made it so good I want to do it again? What else might I try?" And if your children are returning to a piece they began the day before, they might look at it and ask, "What else might I work on today to make this my strongest piece of writing yet?" To support this work during your conferences, you will want to refer to the charts and to their plans. You might ask, "What is your plan for today? What goal are you working on as a writer?" Then you will likely want to help your students set up plans of action for carrying out their self-selected goals.

Revise for elaboration and character. Story-tell to uncover important details and add dialogue to highlight important character traits.

Plan to spend the first portion of this final bend encouraging children to use all they know to write lots of stories, and emphasizing revision. To begin this work, remind students of any revision strategies and tools you taught them during prior writing units this year. Revision, you'll remind them, is a complement to good writing. If they have a small stack of stories that they like, those stories merit being revised. If a child really doesn't like one or two of the books she has written, those texts might not "deserve" revision.

48

Take this time to post the anchor charts from this unit and earlier narrative units around the room for children to refer to. Students can study the charts and think, "What will I work on today? How will I make my piece the very, very best it can be?" Then, with their plans in mind, they can gather the necessary materials from the classroom writing center before diving into their work. Of course, to facilitate this work, you will need to ensure that children have access to the necessary materials. You will likely want to provide them each with a revision folder and a colored pen, swatches of paper on which they can add paragraphs to their drafts, and flaps of paper that can be taped over parts of the story they decide to revise. Teach them to use staple removers, if they don't already use these regularly, so they can make their books longer or shorter.

At this point in their school careers, your writers will be familiar with many purposes of revision, and they will be adept at setting goals for their own revision using the charts. Because it is likely that many children are still summarizing rather than storytelling with detail, highlight that one of the most important reasons for second-graders to revise is to elaborate. If a child wrote, "For Jorge's birthday, he got a bike," teach this child that he can cross out that summary of the event and instead story-tell exactly what happened, step by step. Injunctions to "add more information" or "add details" don't necessarily help writers shift from summarizing to storytelling. Instead, such comments too often lead to pages that contain a lot of summary—pages like this: "For Jorge's birthday, he got a bike. It was red and had a basket. He liked it. He was happy. It was a great, great bike." So coach children to make a movie in their mind, to think, "What did the character say or do exactly?" and to tell the story bit by bit.

For children who are storytelling with detail, you can remind them to build up the tension in the story. For example, instead of writing, "Jorge got a bike," the writer might write, "The box was really big. Jorge closed his eyes and wished. 'Please, please, please let it be a bike,' he thought. 'Go on, open it,' his dad said. Jorge pulled back the top and saw a red thing. Could it be? Then there was a basket. 'A bike!' Jorge yelled. He was happy."

All students can do the same sort of revision with any story. Help them check to be sure they are storytelling, creating little scenes using dialogue and small actions to let the story unfold on the page.

You might teach your students that writers of fiction often use dialogue not just to show what's happening but also to show characters' personalities. Since you can make characters say anything, why not have them say things that show what they are like? A bully wouldn't say, "Pass me the peas, please." She might instead say something like, "Hey, Stupid, hand over the peas!" In a minilesson, you might demonstrate how you reread your writing, revision pen in hand, focusing just on the dialogue and saying to yourself, "Is there something else this character could say that would show his personality?" To help figure out what the character could say and do, you might suggest that kids think of a person in real life who is like the character they are trying to create and imagine what that real person might say. They could also think of a familiar character from a book or a movie.

Revise for meaning.

You might also teach children that it can help to think about the really important life lessons their character learns, and to show those life lessons. Often writers will add something about those lessons as a way to end a story. "From that day on, Anna always remembered that she could take the time to make her grandma happy." "After that, Otto always remembered to keep his toys in his backpack until recess time, and he didn't get in trouble again."

Channel students to try out literary leads and endings that send a message.

You might also teach children to create more literary beginnings or endings. It is useful to show kids that they can try writing a few different versions of a lead or an ending (or any part of their story, for that matter) before deciding which one works best. To broaden their understanding of the various ways published story beginnings and endings are structured, children could study mentor texts the class has read, trying to name what the writer did in the beginning or ending.

As mentioned earlier, you may decide to make endings a big deal. The Common Core State Standards for reading call for children to be able to recount stories and determine their central message or lesson by the end of second grade. You might ask your children to do this same kind of lesson or message work in their writing. Teach children to ask themselves, "What does my story teach other people?" Kids might do this work with a partner. The partners might read each other's writing and then try to jot down what the main character learned—or what they learned. You may want to teach some of your more advanced writers that the lesson and the heart of the story usually go together. You could refer to the incinerator scene in *Toy Story* 3 to help teach this concept. This scene sends the message that friends stick together no matter what.

Have students polish for publication.

As you near the end of this unit, tell children that they will be celebrating soon. To prepare, they should spend some time polishing their writing—capitalizing proper nouns such as names and special places, rereading to ensure that the story remains in a third-person voice, and adding words or punctuation that may have been left out.

Celebrate student writing by reading aloud and having book talks.

Your children will write many pieces during this unit, and you will likely have each child pick one that he or she will publish. Encourage students to reread their pieces to find the one that builds the most tension and/or carries the most significance. Then you might make your celebration an "accountable talk" celebration. Ask your authors to read their stories aloud to the class and then give the class time to talk about these moments. If you have done the message work described in the final bend above, you will be acknowledging especially that their stories are very important. They are so significant, they need to be read and also discussed. In preparation for this, children might practice reading these stories in their best read-aloud voices, slowing down at parts and then reading with excitement at others.

Alternatively, you might set up a time to share the stories with another class or older buddies in another grade. You might even add the stories to your classroom library to be shared year after year. (Your kids could group together the ones with similar messages.) Or each child could think of a place in the classroom or the school where their story might live. For example, stories about getting hurt might live in the nurse's office, or stories about being a new kid at a new school might live in the main office.

Whatever you choose to do with the writing from this unit, your larger message will be that you and your students have worked hard to make this writing stand shoulder to shoulder with the best writing on your classroom's and the school library's bookshelves. Perhaps you'll ask partners to work together, writing blurbs for the back of each other's books to convince people to read them!

Writing Persuasive Reviews

RATIONALE/INTRODUCTION

The Common Core State Standards spotlight the importance of opinion writing, or persuasive writing as it is also called. The invitation to voice their opinions far and wide is appealing to youngsters, who are eager not only to be seen but also to be heard. They'll gladly share opinions about everything from food to movies to video games, and they are skilled at arguing for things they want—a later bedtime, a trip to Disneyland, a new puppy. It's a small step, then, to teach children to channel their opinion writing into the specific genre of persuasive reviews.

As writers progress along a trajectory of opinion/argument writing, they move from writing opinions that are purely personal to ones that are more persuasive and more universal. This unit gives youngsters the power to use their writing to persuade others to believe what they believe and take action as a result of their writing, which is ultimately what the Common Core expects students to do. It conveys to students that they have a voice and that writing can be a great vehicle for sharing what they think with others. It also sets them up for the literary essays they will write later in their school careers.

As with any writing unit, students will write a lot right from the start. In the unit we overview here, students begin writing reviews from the start. You'll be able to see what your students do in Bend I—studying their early reviews—and this will inform how your teaching unfolds. Once your writers have written a number of reviews, they will be able to go back to all those reviews, improving them by applying what they have learned from a careful study of mentor texts. In the third and final bend of the unit, you will ask your writers to look over all the reviews they have written and revised to decide which ones they might polish to share with others.

A SUMMARY OF THE BENDS IN THE ROAD FOR THIS UNIT

In Bend I (Get Kids Started Writing Lots and Lots of Reviews and Living Differently Because They Are Critics), you'll teach students to live like critics, carrying a notepad with them everywhere they go so that during writing workshop they can generate one review after another. The main goal in this part of the unit will be to immerse your students in the wide world of reviews and teach in a way that produces a high volume and high levels of enthusiasm and engagement. Plan to spend a day or so immersing students in persuasive reviews and debate, and then allow three days for them to write their own reviews.

In Bend II (Make Reviews More Persuasive: Add Details and More Specific Language and Use Mentor Texts), your teaching will focus on the qualities of good writing. Through the study of carefully selected mentor texts, you'll teach students strategies for crafting not only well-organized reviews but also detailed, convincing, beautiful pieces of writing. You will also promote independence. On any one day, some children will be revising previously written reviews and some will be writing new ones. You may spend a week in this bend or decide to expand it to two, but don't linger much longer than that.

In Bend III (Get Ready to Share Your Reviews with the World), you'll teach in ways that expand children's skills at editing. Note what they can do without help, and think about how you can help children progress in this arena. If some are not using commas in a list, for example, you can gather these youngsters together and teach that now. If some are not rereading for meaning, or noticing when their writing makes no sense or is overly repetitive, you can lead small-group work to support that. You should dedicate three to four days of teaching and work time to Bend III.

GETTING READY

Gather Texts for Students, as Well as Special Materials

You'll want to gather a variety of reviews to share with your students. Book reviews appear in magazines and are posted online, movie reviews are part of weekly television and radio newscasts, and the local bookstore has travel guides for favorite neighborhood restaurants, shops, and hotels. Invite your kids to begin searching at home for reviews. You might create a drumroll around this unit by displaying the reviews that children collect. You may want to gather children's literature in which characters are persuasive or make extensive arguments. Examples include *Check, Please!* (a book in the *Frankly, Frannie* series, by AJ Stern); *Click, Clack, Moo*, by Doreen Cronin; *Grace for President*, by Kelly DiPucchio; and Mo Willems's Don't Let the Pigeon series and *The Duckling Gets a Cookie*!? You'll save this latter collection of titles for later in the unit, when your focus is not on writing reviews but on being persuasive.

As part of this unit, you may decide to encourage your students to carry a small notepad with them everywhere, jotting down their opinions and recording facts to help with writing their reviews—just like *New York Magazine*'s food critic Adam Platt does. These pads might be made from half sheets of paper with eight or ten lines and perhaps a small box for a sketch, stapled together at the top. You might want to cover the staples with thick tape (colored duct tape if you want to get fancy) to make the binding stronger.

Use Additional Professional Texts as Needed

The small handbook *A Quick Guide to Teaching Persuasive Writing, K–2*, by Sarah Picard Taylor, which is part of the Workshop Help Desk series, can support the work of this unit and provide inspiration for adaptations to meet your specific needs. You could also refer back to the first-grade volume *Writing Reviews* for alternative ideas for mentor texts or lessons.

Choose When and How Children Will Publish

Because the point of persuasive writing is to persuade others, it's important that your students' writing be published in a public way. They are writing to persuade, and you will be spending significant time teaching your students to tailor their writing to a specific audience. Therefore, their writing needs to make it into the hands of the intended audience. Students may chose to deliver their writing to the intended recipient or perhaps post it on a bulletin board where the right people will be able to read it. Perhaps you will enlist the help of your school's media specialist, and students' reviews can be posted online or included in the school newspaper. Whatever you decide, help your students get their opinions out for all to hear.

BEND I: GET KIDS STARTED WRITING LOTS AND LOTS OF REVIEWS AND LIVING DIFFERENTLY BECAUSE THEY ARE CRITICS

Involve students in the process of gathering mentor texts—then immerse them in reading persuasive reviews and noticing characteristics of the genre.

The unit should start off with great momentum and energy. Your students will not want to spend days coming up with one opinion piece, nurturing it slowly, and toiling over drafts and revisions. Because the genesis of this writing lies in children's likes and dislikes, you can encourage your students to generate many opinions and draft many reviews, each one slightly better than the last. We envision your classroom during this unit as a hotbed of debate and talk, with drafts of reviews flying off children's pencils to be read by partners, argued over, and finally revised for publication.

Before the first day of the unit, you might want to begin immersing your students in the wide world of persuasive reviews by reading reviews aloud, sending kids off to search for a range of reviews, and encouraging them to talk (and think) like reviewers throughout the day. You might begin by gathering your kids, perhaps during shared writing or morning meeting, and reminding them how people see reviewers as friends to lean on for advice. Then, you might invite students to prepare for writing their own reviews by brainstorming lists or collecting pictures of things they like or dislike.

As a read-aloud, you can share books like *Check, Please!* (a book in the Frankly, Frannie series by AJ Stern) to show students the power a persuasive writer has over an audience. You might also encourage children to interview adults in their lives to learn how reviews affect grown-ups' decisions. Meanwhile, you'll want to show children that you use reviews as well. Perhaps you'll read aloud a few reviews of books you're thinking of adding to your read-aloud list and help children see how these reviews influence your choices. Tell them how you lean on reviews to find the next movie you want to see or decide which cupcakes to buy for the publishing party.

As you read a sample review aloud, highlight words the reviewer has used, in particular those that express opinions, reasons, or details you think are especially influential, and encourage your kids to use persuasive language as they talk about the texts you have read. Perhaps you'll start a chart for students to refer to to support the use of persuasive language, with such phrases as "This is important because . . . ," "One reason is . . . ," "Another reason is . . . ," and "You should . . ." You might want to start separate charts for useful vocabulary that appears in your read-alouds. Words for best and worst might be displayed along a continuum (*fantastic* on one end, *horrible* on the other, with everything in between listed in a logical order, according to the kids). Reading aloud reviews, searching for reviews in the real world, and practicing persuasive language and vocabulary through shared experiences and conversations may lead up to the unit and continue during it.

Create a shared experience so that students can practice coming up with, and then supporting, an opinion when faced with a differing opinion.

Alternatively, you may want to launch the unit by giving children a shared experience that invites an opinionated response. Perhaps they might taste different kinds of ice cream (be sure to get permission from caretakers for an activity like this). Groups of children who prefer one kind of ice cream can work on shared reviews to promote the flavor they like best. You may want to incorporate debate, suggesting the pro-chocolate group collect their reasons in preparation for the debate, while the pro-vanilla group does the same. The youngsters can learn to brainstorm many possible defenses, to settle on their best, and then to present their side to the opposition. This will help your students see that reviews are not simply "I like this" statements but are actually arguments. A grounding in debate can help children grasp that they need to elaborate on reasons why their opinions are sound and to consider counterarguments.

Then, too, you will also want to remind your students that they've studied persuasive writing in prior years, and can bring all they learned to bear on their reviews. For example, if your students have written persuasive speeches in the past, you might say something like, "Boys and girls, remember when you wrote persuasive speeches? I remember how one of the first-grade classes gave a speech to the custodians to ask for more paper towels in the bathroom. Do you remember what you learned then about how to be persuasive?" You may decide to chart some of these student-generated tips.

Go! Remind students of sources for review ideas, and then get started!

"Now that we've read so many reviews, it's your turn to write to convince others to agree with you about the things you love. You need only think about your favorite things or books or places, then state an opinion and bolster it with precise information that you can dig up from memories and personal experiences."

Eventually, you can complicate this process by teaching them ways to gather information beyond what they already know, but for starters, this work is important in and of itself.

Invite your students to work with zeal and independence, writing one review, then another, and another, collecting each new review in their writing folders. Some will work for half a day on a review, then write another. More of them will work for a day or a day and a half on a review before starting a second one. You definitely do not want them all doing this work in sync under your direction, so that they all crank out one made-to-spec review.

You don't need to divide the whole wide world of reviews up into categories—movie reviews, restaurant reviews, product reviews—and teach each category separately from the rest. Instead, you will want students to pick topics they are passionate and want to influence others about.

If your students are slow to generate topics, you'll want to teach either whole-class or small-group lessons to those who need help with a strategy for doing this. If students are not writing with fluency and volume, you may decide to use a timer and call out prompts: "By now, your hand should be flying down the page." "By now, you should have written half a page." You may need to gather a small group to nudge them into writing more quickly and closely observe them to understand what is slowing them down.

Live life as a reviewer: teach students to be aware of their opinions and on the lookout for facts to support them.

Once your children are writing reviews, you will start teaching them as intensely and directly as possible. There is no one strategy to teach first. One possible place to begin is by teaching them that they should find themselves living differently because they are now reviewers, seeing their lives as rehearsal for writing. To support the idea that people who write reviews walk through life as critics, you may want to teach students that they can carry a small notepad with them everywhere, jotting down their opinions and recording the specific facts that will enhance their reviews. The children can carry these notepads around with them to jot notes about school lunch, the local pizza place after school, and the movie they rented for the weekend.

Go back to basics: teach students to organize and plan opinion writing, angling their reviews toward their audience.

As students begin to gather up opinions everywhere they go, you will probably want to remind them of a few of the basics of opinion writing. Many students will have learned these basics in first grade when writing speeches, letters, or reviews. If your students have not written speeches, reviews, or any type of persuasive writing before now however, you'll want to introduce these basics afresh. Perhaps the most essential concept to communicate is the fact that a reviewer not only states his or her opinion but also provides reasons to back up that opinion. You might suggest your young reviewers use a booklet to organize their writing, stating their opinion clearly on the first page, and then dividing each of the following pages to other supporting reasons (you can tuck into this lesson that usually there are at least three or four reasons to support a strong opinion). Then you could suggest writers include at least a simple concluding sentence on the final page. Once the basic structure is there, you'll also want to teach your students to elaborate on their reasons. For example, if a child is writing, "I like Ben & Jerry's Chocolate Fudge Brownie the best of all chocolate ice creams," you can teach him to elaborate on the reasons. Instead of "One reason is that it has brownies," he might say, "One reason I like Chocolate Fudge Brownie the best is that it has little chunks of brownie in it. The brownie is so tasty! The brownie chunks are nice and small, and there are just the right amount in each bite." The details help.

As you near the end of the first bend, you might revisit the importance of planning, reminding students that they can touch each page as they say what will go there, just as they did when they wrote narratives, or that they can practice with a partner to get what they want to say planned out before they write down every word. In a minilesson, a fully developed teaching point might sound like this: "Writers, I want to teach you that when writing reviews, it helps if the review sounds like you are talking to the reader. For this to happen, try saying in your mind what you are going to write. You can touch the part of the page on which you might be writing and say out loud what you plan to write before putting the words on the page." After ten or fifteen minutes of quiet writing time have passed, you might add to this minilesson with a mid-workshop teaching point, saying, "Writers know it can help to reread their draft, thinking 'How will this affect readers?' If you want some help imagining a reader's response to your writing, you can ask your writing partner to be your reader and to tell you what he or she is thinking." You can suggest partners help not only by giving responses and suggestions, but also by asking writers to consider alternatives, saying things like, "Is there a better or more convincing way to say that? Try again." "Say it like you are trying to convince a grown-up."

If you want your children to think about persuading an audience, you might teach them that it helps to clarify who that audience is. You might say, "Reviewers think to themselves, 'Am I writing the review for a grown-up or a kid? Are my readers music lovers, other avid readers, expert game players, or pizza fanatics?'" You might add the tip: "Sometimes when you are writing your reviews, your audience can be wide and varied. You may be trying to convince lots of different people. You want to make sure you write in ways that include everyone. For example, you can say, 'Not only is it great for kids, but parents will love it too because . . .'"

You can use the anticipated audience to ramp up the level of children's reviews. For example, if you find that your students become so jazzed about all the possible topics that they rush in their writing folder, you might say, "Writers, do you remember that when you wrote your how-to books, you made sure to include all the things your reader needed to know? Well, when writing reviews, you also need to think about your reader. Today, I want to teach you that it can be helpful to reread each review before you start a new one. Writers reread and find places where they may have left out an idea. Then they quickly pick up their pens and add to the review so their readers will be convinced by what they have to say."

BEND II: MAKE REVIEWS MORE PERSUASIVE: ADD DETAILS AND MORE SPECIFIC LANGUAGE AND USE MENTOR TEXTS

Plan a guided inquiry that allows students to examine and notice features of persuasive reviews.

As children continue writing up a storm, you'll add instruction—via mentor reviews, explicit teaching, conferences, and small-group work—that lifts the level of their work. In the first bend, you will have taught students to live as critics, seeing potential reviews everywhere and understanding that it's important to capture precise details: the name of the pizza that tasted so good, the awards the terrific movie won, a description of the amazing opening number at the dance exhibition. In a similar way, it will be important to teach youngsters that as writers of reviews, they need to read reviews differently, asking, "How did the writer go about making this?" and "What does this reviewer do that I could try as well?" That is, you'll remind children that just as they can learn from mentor authors of narratives, they can learn from mentor authors of reviews.

To kick off the study of mentor texts, you might choose a review to enlarge or place on a document camera and invite students to talk with a partner about what they notice. Take note of what comes easily to your students, as well as what they do not notice. For example, did your students notice that the writer used sensory details to help the reader make a picture in her mind? If they didn't, you might plan to teach this more explicitly the next day. In any case, one way to proceed is to begin with an inquiry. Ask the students what they notice, then follow up with explicit minilessons that name some of the strategies the mentor authors were using.

Of course, if your students are still getting the hang of the basic organization of reviews (stating the opinion clearly, naming three or four supports, providing a simple conclusion), you may find yourself needing to use the study of mentor texts as a vehicle for teaching the basics of opinion writing. They may need you to linger a bit longer on the idea that a reviewer not only states his or her opinion but also provides reasons to back up that opinion. Using examples from mentor texts, you might teach students who do not already seem to know that it is important to state the reasons they are recommending something and then elaborate on those reasons. For instance, if a child is writing, "I like Roma's pizza the best," you might first teach him to make sure he writes down why that is true.

Encourage students to come up with relevant details by using their senses and studying artifacts and mentor texts.

Many of your students will write claims such as "Roma's pizza is the best," and then, as they proceed through their persuasive writing, they'll dedicate each page of their booklet to one reason why that pizza is the best. On one page, the writer may suggest it is the best because the owners are friendly and then provide details. On another page, the writer may say that the pizza is the best for another reason and again provide supporting details. There are many ways a writer can make these details more compelling and vivid.

One thing you will want to help children notice is that to really affect a reader, it generally helps to write with details. This is true in narrative writing and true also in persuasive writing. You can teach children that writers select and add details that convey what they want to convey. So if a child wants to convey that the pizza is delicious, the child might write about the steaming hot cheese that oozes over the edge of the pizza. You might say, "As you revise your old reviews and also write new ones, you'll want to make sure that your reader gets a clear picture. To help readers envision something, writers use lots of details and precise language. Writers use their senses to describe the atmosphere of a place, the smell, taste, texture, and even the sound of food. Writers sometimes even try some show, not tell, to describe the way songs, books, and movies make them feel."

You might gather small groups of students to teach a range of strategies for writing with detail. One group of students might learn that when writing details, one thing they can do is look back at artifacts, such as restaurant menus, movie tickets, playbills, or video game guidebooks, to spark a memory of the experience they had and then add those specific details to the review. Another group working on writing with detail might learn a different strategy—that it is helpful to look at other reviews on the same (or a similar) topic to notice the things that other critics write in their reviews. They can look to these mentor critics and think about the things they can add or try in their own writing. You might then guide this group to notice that the kinds of details depend on the topic. Food reviewers usually include flavors, textures, and the presentation of food, as well as the chef's name. Restaurant reviewers include information about the menu offerings, service, cleanliness, ambiance, and price. Video game reviewers describe the graphics, sound effects, and skill level needed to play. Book reviewers describe the characters, summarize the plot, and talk about the way the author writes. A third group learning to write with better detail might learn that sometimes it is helpful to draw a detailed picture on each page showing one reason for an opinion, complete with labels and captions, then write out the sentences of the review, making sure that all the details in the pictures are also in the words.

Introduce sticky notes as a tool to support revision work.

As children learn to add details, they'll need room on the page to fit all this new information. To support this work, you may want to help children learn to use sticky notes. Kids can number the sticky notes to match the revision places in their reviews. Using sticky notes makes revisions more inviting and much neater, since it's easier to incorporate the revisions into the published piece. It might be helpful to teach students that sometimes writers need to leave themselves a note or give themselves the job of finding more information about their subject. For example, they may need to look up the price of an item, the name of an author, or the spelling of a character's name. Kids can use sticky notes to remind them to find more information.

Teach students to elaborate by using thought prompts, choosing relevant details, and including small moments.

As students join you in studying effective reviews, you'll want to be ready to point out some of the strategies that will pay off for them. First, the writer can elaborate, providing more substantiating information and using an authoritative voice. To teach writers to do this, you can always lean on the prompts to push thinking that you have taught or that students may have been taught in prior years. Prompts that could especially help reviewers elaborate more are "This is important because . . . " "The reason for this is . . . " "This shows that . . . because . . . " With all these tools in hand, your students will be writing powerfully persuasive pages like this: "Roma's pizza is awesome because the pizza is never greasy. The reason for this is they use real olive oil, not cooking grease. This is important because grease is really bad for you."

Another way for students to improve their writing is by elaborating with more powerful material. For example, you might help them notice that carefully chosen details affect readers. You might remind children that earlier, in narrative writing, they learned that details matter. Do they also see this in the reviews they are studying? Chances are that any well-written or persuasive review will contain carefully chosen details. You'll want to channel children to look back at all the reviews they have written thus far in the unit—and they may have produced half a dozen by now—and think, "How could I rewrite these reviews so that I include details that are going to persuade my readers?" The child who wants to convey that the pizza is delicious might write about the chunks of sausage that sit on the steaming hot cheese. You might teach your students—all of them or just the more proficient—that the secret is not only to choose details that make one's case but also to choose words that have the right connotation. The pizza may have a slick pool of grease on its surface, but that won't be a detail to highlight. Remember, if you teach this to writers, they'll then return to their folders (or notebooks) full of reviews and put this new lesson into action by revising those reviews. You'll decide whether these revisions require an entirely new draft or can be accomplished with flaps, arrows, insertions, and the like.

Of course, the details need to be relevant. You may want to remind children in whole-class instruction that reviewers tend to have in mind the sorts of things that are important to describe, whether they are writing about a book, a movie, or a restaurant. Once students have discerned what different reviewers usually focus on—for instance, that food critics tend to talk about presentation and movie critics often comment on the leading lady's costume—your classroom will be bursting with experts of all sorts, using language like, "I could add some more about the service," or "I haven't said anything about the different appetizers yet." You might want to encourage student partnerships to refer to charts listing these techniques as they reread their reviews and look for ways to add more and be more persuasive.

Students can also make their reviews more persuasive if they tuck small anecdotes about their subjects into the review. Students can use what they learned from the personal narrative and realistic fiction units of study to craft tight narratives that illustrate the example they are using. The food critic may tell the story of the friendly waiter who delivered special straws shaped like flamingos for the kids to illustrate the high quality of service at the restaurant. As they craft these small anecdotes, you may want to teach children to remember all they know about strong narrative writing: zooming in on a small moment; including dialogue, action, and feelings; and showing instead of telling feelings. You might teach students to angle their anecdotes by picking and choosing which part of the story to "pop out." In a minilesson you might say, "Writers, today I want to teach you that when you want to be more convincing, sometimes it helps to add details to the most important parts of the mini-story. You might go back and add these details into a review you already wrote, or you might start a new review and plan to add those details." (See pages 31–33 in *A*

Quick Guide to Teaching Persuasive Writing, K–2, to see how a teacher used a first-grade writer's letter to show how she made a clear picture for the reader with a little mini-story.)

Teach children that review writers have a logical, organizing structure to their writing.

Another way to lift the level of students' reviews is to help them develop an organizing structure into which their reasons will fit. This sort of revision will be the most dramatic of all and will almost certainly require that writers write an entirely new draft. It may be, then, that you ask students to select their best review and do this more extensive work on just that review.

To do this, students will need to make a claim—"Roma's pizza is the best"—think about possible reasons they can cite to support the claim, and choose reasons that go together. For example, one child might say, "From the time I entered the door till the time I took my first bite, I knew Roma's pizza was the best. When I first entered the restaurant, the people were so friendly. Then when I sat down, the service was so good. But the best thing happened when my food arrived—the pizza was delicious." The writer might then gather evidence and little stories to show that the people were friendly and then write another section just about the great service.

Show your writers exemplars of opinion writing to help them notice how related evidence is grouped together with common transition phrases (*for example, also*). To do this, you might use the opinion learning progression and/or the work of previous students. All of this work is essential to the Common Core State Standards for opinion writing, which expect students to "introduce the topic . . . , state an opinion, and create an organizational structure that lists reasons"; to "provide reasons that support an opinion"; and to "use linking words and phrases to connect opinions and reasons."

Teach students to consider audience when doing revision work.

Yet another way for students to elaborate on their reviews is to continue to keep an audience in mind. If they can visualize their readers, they can craft sentences with language tailored to that audience. If the review is about the second *Cars* movie, the student needs to determine whether he is writing his review for people who have seen only the first *Cars* movie or both movies. If the audience has seen both movies, then the writer may choose to compare and contrast, saying which movie is better or how they differ in important ways.

Reviewers can also build their own credibility by writing something like, "I eat pizza at least twice a week and I believe that Gino's is by far the best place around to get plain cheese pizza." Others make the review seem trustworthy by quoting an expert. Writers often try out different introductions and pick the introduction that sounds most impressive or persuasive to their audience.

You may decide to tuck these ideas into a revision minilesson that supports kids revising their introductions or conclusions. Showing your students options for beginning or ending their reviews, charting the possibilities with mentor texts nearby, and providing choice will be important. You can then teach students to revise their endings by providing conclusions that sum up their opinions, recommending similar books or restaurants if the opinion is positive or perhaps directing readers or diners to a better book or restaurant if the opinion is negative. A star rating system or other ranking code invented by your young critics can also be added to the end of the review.

Push your students to even higher levels: teach counterargument and paragraphing and introduce lined paper.

For stronger writers who have mastered some or all of the basic persuasive structures, you may want to introduce the counterargument as a way to bump up the level of their thinking and writing. Although this doesn't appear in the opinion writing section of the Common Core State Standards until later years, the third-grade reading standards expect children to be able to distinguish their own viewpoint from that of the author of a nonfiction text. You might therefore reasonably expect (or teach) students who are eager for more that they can entertain the possibility of another point of view on their topic and write a bit about that as a way to air the other side of the argument. You might reasonably expect, for example, that your students understand that their favorite pizza place is not the favorite of all their friends. Reviewers, you might teach them, try to include other perspectives in their reviews to show that they know there are other opinions out there. So an added paragraph in a review might begin, "Not everyone feels this way about Roma's. Some people say that the crust is too thin. Some complain that you always have to wait in line." Then you can teach them that reviewers always like to get the last word in, so the paragraph might end, "But I still think Roma's crusts are worth waiting for!"

You will want to remind students that in expository writing, the pages, or paragraphs, serve different purposes from those in narrative writing. Whereas in stories paragraphs change to indicate that time is passing or the setting is changing or a new character is present, in opinion writing paragraphs change to show the reader that different evidence will be presented, that the opinion writer is moving to another thought that nevertheless still connects to the main idea.

You'll notice some of your students choosing paper with more and more lines, and you might see that some begin combining the material from two pages onto one page, with either a space as a divider or an indent. Once they are successfully doing this independently, you might consider offering sheets of regular lined notebook paper for some students in place of booklets. Of course, if lined paper seems to send kids back to simply listing their reasons, or writing in a run-on, disorganized, off-the-top-of-the-head way, then booklets, with their inherent organizational qualities, are a far better option.

BEND III: GET READY TO SHARE YOUR REVIEWS WITH THE WORLD

Guide students as they select a persuasive review to publish. Which idea do they want to get out into the world? Which piece of writing can benefit from revision?

Once children have been writing for a few weeks and have drafted and revised lots of reviews, it's time for them to choose one or more pieces to publish. There are a number of optional ways to publish that you might consider, from simply posting the reviews around the school or neighborhood to getting fancy with video or the Internet. In any case, you will want to teach your students to sort through their folders full of reviews and choose the ones they want to put out into the world. In a minilesson, you will want to encourage your writers to choose wisely and to be open to revision. Instead of asking them to choose pieces to *publish*, you might say, "Today, I want to teach you that writers choose their best work for *revision*. If a writer thinks, 'I'm completely done with this review, there is not one thing I want to change,' that is not the right piece to choose for publishing. Writers choose pieces they want to revise."

When it comes to publishing reviews, you can offer choices to your kids, sharing that when reviewers want their ideas to reach lots of people, they will publish a review on the Internet, in an anthology of similar kinds of reviews, or in the local newspaper. Other writers only want to persuade a small audience; after reading a spectacular book, a writer may write to her closest friend to recommend the book and tell her friend the reasons she should read it. The same writer may also choose to write to the author of the book to tell him why the book was so great. Likewise, students may decide to write a persuasive letter to the owner of the local pizzeria or may work with like reviewers to create an anthology of restaurant reviews. As you and the kids discover qualities of effective reviews—persuasive reviews—you'll be encouraging children to revise the dozen or so draft reviews they have already written, and you'll teach them to incorporate all they are learning in more ambitious plans for the new reviews they are writing.

Teach students to revise with the lens of making their writing as persuasive as it can be.

In the final days of the unit, you might say to your kids, "As we get ready to share these reviews with the world, we must do more revision work. Today I want to teach you that when writers reread to revise their reviews, they often think about taking away parts that don't support their claims. They ask themselves, 'Do I have any details that don't support my idea?' and then they cross those parts out." You will probably need to remind your students that they already have a toolbox full of revision strategies that they know how to use. You might highlight the charts the class developed together when they studied mentor texts, as well as charts from past units that might support their revision work in this unit.

As kids revise their pieces, you might also consider teaching a minilesson that reminds them not to simply make revisions for revision's sake but to keep their eyes on the prize. The larger goal of the unit is to be persuasive. You might say, "Today, I want to teach you that we choose the strategies that will make our writing more persuasive. When you reread to revise your reviews, think, 'Should I add more reasons to express my opinion? Should I envision the scene and add more descriptive details to give a clearer picture? Should I add more specific details?' Then decide which strategies to use to make your review more persuasive."

Teach strategies for making writing readable. Readers can't be persuaded if they can't read what you have to say.

After several days of hefty revision, when most of your children have tried several beginnings and endings and have tried out various techniques for making their reviews as persuasive as possible, it will be time to edit. You'll probably need to help kids understand that editing is very different from revising. Revising means making big, sweeping, important changes to the piece of writing. Editing means cleaning it up a bit, proofreading it for mechanics and the like, making it easier for others to read. This stage of the writing process is the perfect opportunity to help students transfer all they have been learning about grammar and mechanics to their own writing. It's important that you ensure that all your kids have the opportunity to do this work independently. Nobody should be "correcting" the students' work for them; this should be their best approximation. They are expected to edit their work on their own, just as they drafted and revised it on their own. You might begin by reminding students that they have been working hard to make their reviews convincing for the reader, and so they will want to be sure that others are able to read what they have written. You might remind students to use their editing checklists as they reread their reviews. They can check to see that all the word wall words are spelled correctly, that they have used their best spelling, that their sentences, as well as any proper nouns or titles, begin with capital letters, and that they have ended each sentence with punctuation that makes sense.

Of course, students can also use conventions in crafty or meaningful ways. You might remind them that another thing to think about when getting ready to publish their writing is words, phrases, or titles that they want to emphasize or make the reader notice. For instance, we use boldface type, underlining, italics, and exclamation points to show parts that are important. Kids (like their adult reviewer counterparts) might also want to use real photographs or rating systems like three stars or five doughnuts.

Lastly, an investigation of the words used to hold a text together seems important at this juncture. The Common Core State Standards expect second-graders to be able to "use linking words and phrases to connect opinions and reasons." The perfect time to teach this is while students are revising or editing their opinion pieces. You will want to teach children to use vocabulary to signal agreement (*in addition, furthermore*), to compare or contrast a viewpoint (*however, on the other hand*), or to interject (*or, yet*).

Publish the Reviews

Writers often study what other reviewers have done to gather inspiration for how to publish their own work. You might encourage your students to publish their reviews on popular review websites, in "gamer" magazines, or in the school newspaper. Positive reviews can be handed to store owners or waitresses. School bulletin boards can guide students to different local establishments or popular games or warn students not to spend money on products they probably won't like. Another option is for students to videotape themselves delivering "infomercials" based on their reviews and have other students watch the tape and reveal whether they were persuaded. Amazon, Zappos, and other popular shopping websites now include short video reviews of many of their products that could be used as inspiration for how your students might publish and present their work from this unit.

Independent Writing Projects Across the Genres

RATIONALE/INTRODUCTION

This unit is the perfect send-off for children who are almost-third-graders. It is meant as a celebration and acknowledgment of all that they have learned this year. This unit is an invitation to kids to write in a genre that the class has studied together over the year or to apply what they have learned about good writing to new genres that may intrigue and interest them.

Skilled writers have a repertoire of genres in which they work, and they have an aware-ness of how each genre is its own particular tool to make a message strong and meaningful. If second-graders are to become more powerful writers, it is important for them to know their audience, to understand the purpose of their message, and to be able to choose the genre that best communicates their message.

Once your second-graders can work inside a genre that you select for them using the mentors you provide, and can write effectively, it is a small leap for those same children to do that kind of writing with greater independence. This unit will breathe new life into your writing workshop, it will infuse genre studies with greater purpose and meaning throughout the month, and it will set children up to orchestrate all that they know to write with independence.

Mandates, Tests, Standards

The Common Core State Standards expect that children will learn the skills and strate-gies they need to know to write any type of text. Beginning in kindergarten, children are expected to have the foundations to write narrative, opinion, and informational/procedural texts and to develop their writing through their knowledge of the writing process.

The Common Core State Standards also expect second-graders to be able to "focus on a topic and strengthen writing as needed by revising and editing" (W.2.5). Writing partnerships and work with peers in the publishing houses described in this unit teach kids how to meet this standard. In addition, this unit helps children realize that writers choose genres with intent. That is, writers consider their purpose and audience, and then choose the kind of writing that best matches this purpose and audience. As children consider their own choice of genre, they are meeting (and exceeding) Common Core Standards for Reading, including "Identify[ing] the main purpose of a text, including what the author wants to answer, explain, or describe" (RI.2.6).

By now, your children have had exposure to and practice writing in several genres. Even if they have successfully written in this variety of genres, chances are, they may not have a complete understanding of how each one can be a powerful tool. This unit will be essential in supporting kids in becoming purposeful, self-initiated writers.

A SUMMARY OF THE BENDS IN THE ROAD FOR THIS UNIT

In Bend I (Get Started with Writing Projects in a Range of Genres: Generate Ideas, Plan, and Draft), students will self-select the type of writing that they want to study. They will need to recall everything they know about that genre of writing to help guide them to generate ideas, plan, and draft. Students who are working in the same genre will band together with others working in that same genre, creating publishing houses that offer genre-specific support. As the month progresses, your students may want to try out different genres, and so the publishing houses will come to include both writers who are now "experienced" in that genre and writers who are newer to it.

In Bend II (Lift the Quality of Writing), students will focus on the habits, processes, and qualities of good writing within the specific genre in which they are writing to help them lift the level of their work. They will also turn to partnerships within their publishing houses. They'll revise in ways that strengthen their writing. Plan to spend a week in Bend II.

In Bend III (Use Mentor Texts as Personal Writing Teachers), students will use the strategy of consulting mentor texts as writing teachers to further strengthen their writing. They will read these texts in search of parts that resonate with them, study those parts closely to understand what the author has done to achieve a particular effect, and then attempt to replicate those techniques to raise the quality of their own work.

In Bend IV (Prepare for Publication), students will continue with independence, selecting a piece for publishing and thinking about what that piece really needs to make it the best that it can be. Then, independently and within a partnership, students will edit their pieces, paying close attention to the conventions of grammar and the conventions of capitalization, punctuation, and spelling. This week will end with a writing celebration.

GETTING READY

Gather Texts for Students

If there are genres that are new to your children, you may want to consider reading some selections for read-aloud several days before the official launching of the unit. You may want to compile (or recruit children to compile) a few examples of a wide variety of genres. For example, you might want to show youngsters that writers can make any of these (or a few) kinds of text:

- Song books
- Poetry
- Informational books
- Newspaper articles
- Persuasive letters and reviews
- Posters
- Pamphlets
- Greeting cards
- Graphic novels
- Comic books
- Picture books
- Chapter books

Use Additional Professional Texts—and Student Work—as Needed

You may also want to consult professional resources and draw on the work of the children in your classroom. Workshop teaching is most powerful when you respond and teach to your kids' successes and struggles. Because your students have had the opportunity to write in many, if not all, of the genres that you are including in this final unit, you may want to go back and consult the writing that they have generated throughout the year. By being attentive to student work you'll be able to fine-tune your teaching. The work your students do is not just showing you what they can or can't do; it is also showing you what you can do. You could also look to *Independent Writing*, by Colleen Cruz (2004) and *Assessing Writers*, by Carl Anderson (2005) as additional professional resources.

Choose When and How Children Will Publish

As this will be the final publishing ceremony for the entire year, you'll probably want it to be a big deal. You may want to display children's work in a "museum" of writing. Displays could include evidence of children's process, along with their published pieces. Children can explain their choices of genre and publication to visitors. Another idea is to set up a "bookstore" with separate sections for each genre. There could be an area for author readings and posters advertising, "Meet the Author." However you decide to celebrate, you will want to make time for children to reflect on what they have learned about themselves as writers and to make goals for the summer.

BEND I: GET STARTED WITH WRITING PROJECTS IN A RANGE OF GENRES: GENERATE IDEAS, PLAN, AND DRAFT

Rally children around self-selected projects and establish genre-based "publishing houses" to support these.

Gather your youngsters together and tell them that, for the upcoming month, they'll have a chance to invent their own writing projects. This is a departure from what you've been doing with children all year, and it's a significant step toward independence for your now almost-third-graders. You'll want to create a big drumroll. Say something like, "All year, I've been setting us up to do one kind of writing or another, right? Well, guess what? Now it is your turn to decide. It's your turn to come up with your own ideas for the sort of writing you'd like to do. Each one of you will get to pick the kind of writing you'll do as you end second grade."

Once children have decided on the kind of writing they want to make, you can channel them to different publishing houses, with each publishing house representing one kind of genre. So all kids writing narratives will form a narrative publishing house, all kids writing poems will form a poetry publishing house, all kids writing persuasive texts will form a persuasive text publishing house, and so on. In their publishing houses, children will be working side by side with others to make high-quality writing in the genre of their choice, sitting at the same table, sharing mentor texts, and giving each other tips to make their writing stronger.

Before you issue this invitation, think a bit about the choices you hope children will make because, of course, it is easy to steer children. Do you hope your students will reflect on all the kinds of writing you have studied together and select one of those kinds of writing? Or do you hope children will pore over texts that they find in their world, thinking, "I could write just like that!"? They could write adaptations of the types of texts they find most fascinating. Some of your students might be fans of *Star Wars*, for example. Other children love to hear spooky, scary stories late at night. They could write those, too! Do you hope some children will take on a cause—say, convincing the school to spruce up the playground—and that they'll write to make a real-world difference? There are many possibilities, even ones your children may not consider without your guidance. Therefore, take some time to think through your priorities and imagine all the options. Of course, just because you hope children will gravitate toward your genre choices for them doesn't mean that they won't have their own wonderful suggestions. Be prepared to listen to your kids and to adjust your vision based on what they are yearning to write. On the other hand, this unit will work best if children work not alone in a genre, but with other kids, and it will be tricky to oversee too many publishing houses, so do keep an eye on how many different genres kids sign up for, and plan to limit it to a manageable number, perhaps steering children wanting to write in a genre no other child has selected to one that comes close to that, which other children have adopted.

Then too, teaching children to develop ideas that matter to them and to write (perhaps in new formats) about things that they understand and have experienced is a critical part of this unit. Every decision that a writer makes ultimately depends upon her relationship to the idea about which she is writing. You will therefore want to help children select topics that inspire them but that they also know something about based on either firsthand experience or research. The child wanting to write about hiking Mt. Everest might instead write about a mountain she has climbed or might be channeled to engage in research. That is, you may need to rein in—or redirect—children's imaginations just a little.

Remind children of what they have learned about the writing process across the years and launch them into writing.

After rallying children around this idea of self-selected writing, remind them of what they already know how to do. This might sound something like, "Writers, you already know so much about writing. You know how to come up with ideas for your writing and choose paper. You know how to plan and you know that you don't have to wait until you get close to publishing to start the important work of revising. And you know how to make writing easy to read by editing for spelling, capitalization, and punctuation. You will use all of this to make all your own decisions—from topic choice to paper choice. You will decide how your writing will look, what your writing will sound like, and where in the library your writing will go." Keep in mind that this unit is all about the writing process and helping children move through the process with independence and resolve. You will want to bring out a chart of the writing process and put it in a central location or create individual process charts to go into student folders, and to show children how they can keep track of their movement through each step of the process.

In a way, it will be as if you start the unit by making a small keynote address to your writers on that same day, you will want to launch your children into the actual work of independent writing. This means that you will guide them as they generate a topic, choose or create their own paper, plan out how their story or poem or how-to or letter will go, and get started writing. You might want to say, "Ask yourself, 'What do I want my writing to look like? Do I want it to be a chapter book? A comic strip? A picture book?' Turn and tell your partner what you have in mind for your writing project."

Support independence as children make choices around their projects.

One of the ultimate goals that you have for all your students is to become self-directed, deliberate, and confident writers who are deeply engaged because they have taken ownership over their writing. This unit, with its focus on student-selected genres, supports this kind of autonomy.

Students' first step will be to choose (or design) the kind of paper that makes sense for the writing projects they each have in mind. Children who want to write graphic novels might choose blank paper, folding it several times to create boxes for each scene. If you have writers who have decided to write picture books, show them how to staple several pieces of white paper together, drawing a picture box at the top (or bottom) and leaving room for lots of writing. Children who want to create a chapter book could take a handful of paper and fold it in half, so it looks like a series book. This might be a time to include some fancy materials from art so that kids have access to different colors and media if they choose to make cards or pamphlets.

Remind your kids that although all writers always take time to plan for writing, some projects require a little bit more time for planning than others.

BEND II: LIFT THE QUALITY OF WRITING

Expect volume to go up and quality to go down. Reiterate the characteristics of good writing cross genres.

You may find that children are so excited about choosing their genre that their volume goes up drastically but that meanwhile there is, at first, a dip in the quality. You need not worry. As Carl Anderson wrote in *Assessing Writers* (2005), when children "lose control" of their writing, it is often a sign that they are trying out more sophisticated techniques. This is where your teaching becomes the lifeline of this unit. Clearly, since all children will be working inside a different genre, the work of this unit becomes teaching—and oftentimes, reinforcing—the habits, processes, and qualities of good writing that your students work on each and every day in writing workshop.

Then, too, you'll want to remind children that the characteristics of good writing are fairly stable across genres. Whether a child is writing directions or songs, it is equally important to write with precise, exact words, to reread to make sure the meaning is clear, and to answer readers' questions. You might pull out old charts and exemplar texts to remind children to "show, not tell"—in other words, to write in ways that provide their readers with a crystal clear picture of what is happening.

Bolster students' writing in self-selected partnerships.

Since children will be grouped by genre, you may suggest that each child find a partner within his or her publishing house. Although partners will presumably come from within their respective publishing houses, you may want to allow a bit of time for children writing in different genres to compare similar crafting techniques that they have effectively used.

Over the course of this unit, your students will have ample opportunities to practice responding to feedback from peers and adding details to strengthen their writing as needed, which is an end-of-the-year expectation the Common Core holds for second-graders. You will want to remind children of all they know about what makes a good partnership conversation, ways partners help each other during different stages of the writing process, and how partners encourage each other to stay focused on goals. Project partners might decide when and where to meet and how often.

Of course, by this point in the year, you will expect children to be adept at talking about their pieces with one another and giving each other compliments and feedback. Remind them to be specific—pointing to and naming a particular strategy the writer used well and proposing a next step. As you assess the partner work that will be critical to their projects, teach children how to read each other's writing as readers. Writers could gather together, Post-its in hand, read their pieces, and then provide feedback.

Foster revision by making sure that all prior charts and revision tools are made available to students.

You'll want to coach children to use the revision strategy charts in your classroom, which you have probably been adding to all year, as well as the Information, Opinion, and Narrative checklists to help each other revise their writing. Teach them to ask questions as they sit side by side, using the charts and checklists as a reference. For instance, one partner might say, "You used setting details in the lead of your story. Are there any other places where you could try the same thing?" Also, when it comes to improving the quality of writing, you will probably remind your second-graders to get out their revision tools. Flaps and strips, thin markers, Post-its, extra pages, carets, and asterisks are all signals that your kids are going back into their writing to try to make it better. In this unit, you will find it especially helpful to lean on these very concrete symbols of revision to help make sure your children are working on quality, as well as quantity, in their writing.

One surefire way to ignite new energy for revision is to let children know that writers sometimes revise by looking at their material and thinking, "What else could I make of this?" Just as Degas revised his drawings of ballet dancers to be etchings, pastels, paintings, and sculptures, kids can take that favorite story about making pizza with Abuela and revise it to become a poem to Abuela, or a how to make pizza book.

Give students flexibility in genre choice to bring out their emerging writing identities.

One of the great joys of this unit will be the fact that children will emerge as different writers because no two writers will be working on the same exact thing. Even children who are working in the same genre will tend to produce their own versions of that kind of writing, especially with some encouragement from you. Now is a time to take risks. Perhaps one child will write a funny rhyming poem, while another child will write a more serious prose-like poem. You might even encourage your strong writers to create projects that blend genres: a how-to pamphlet that tells kids how to do something good for the environment, like recycle or compost, or a mystery that begins with a cryptic chant (song). Encourage your children to explore and have fun.

You will definitely want to capitalize on children's emerging writing identities. If one child writes a gigantic book of jokes and another writes a screenplay, let each child become famous for what he or she has done, developing an identity as a particular and unique kind of writer. You may want to develop a chart that celebrates every child's expertise. Children can add to this themselves, coming up with interesting ways of describing the work they've mastered.

As the unit progresses, and students decide to try out different and perhaps new genres, the publishing houses will change in structure, with some kids now functioning as experts and others as newcomers. Encourage those kids who have had recent practice in a particular genre to act as mentors. This way, not only will they support newer members of the publishing house, but they will also have a sense of having mastered a genre (even if, in fact, they have just learned the basics!).

BEND III: USE MENTOR TEXTS AS PERSONAL WRITING TEACHERS

Recall ways to write under the guidance of a mentor text, and begin anew.

By this time in the year, your children will have had several experiences using mentor texts. It's time to let them have a go at this work on their own! Teach children to draw from all that they learned in *Lessons from the Masters: Improving Narrative Writing* (and from other units in which they studied mentor authors). That is, children will look to their favorite authors to find—and then try—craft moves that inspire them. Add to their repertoire by teaching children that when writers want to write in a specific genre, they find books to support this work, pick an author that inspires them, and have a go.

You might say, "Writers, you already know how writing teachers live all around us—I am one of your writing teachers, your partner is one of your writing teachers, your publishing house is a whole community of teachers, and the authors that we studied in February are your writing teachers, too. In this new bend of our genre study unit, you will continue that relationship. Choose any author that inspires you to write this new kind of book. If you are the kind of writer who wants to write a spooky, scary story that just scares the pants off of someone, check out *There's a Nightmare in My Closet* by Mercer Mayer. If you're the kind of writer who wants to tell your story with pictures and words, you could study *Silly Lilly and the Four Seasons* by Agnes Rosenstiehl. Or maybe you want to write talking-animal stories like Mo Willems's Elephant and Piggie books. Writers, the possibilities, like your ideas for books and stories and other pieces of writing, are endless."

As children begin this work, remind them that when using mentor texts to find ideas for their writing, they need to first notice a part they like. Once they have that part, they then seek to name the specific craft move the writer used and figure out how the writer did it. Finally, your writers can try this same craft move in their own writing, by selecting a part in their work where it would be beneficial to incorporate that same move. Students need not wait for you to teach them all about different genres then. They can instead rely on the mentor texts to function as teachers. To prepare for this, you might consider creating some new baskets in your library for the books you anticipate children will want to write.

Collect and record genre-specific traits and work that models them.

You could ask children to write lists of what they are noticing and understanding about a particular genre. Those lists can ultimately turn into charts with examples of kids' writing. As students meet in their publishing houses they can use their lists to generate charts that name the characteristics of that particular genre.

Putting examples of how a child has used that in her writing is also a way to generate ownership and a great deal of conversation. "Daisy's group is working on persuasive letters, and Daisy understands and has used transitional phrases. In her letter to her mom about adopting a dog from a shelter she writes, 'Another reason for adopting a dog from a shelter is that it might save the dog's life.' Daisy is showing in her writing that she understands an important characteristic of persuasive writing: the use of transitional phrases."

Teach toward independence and intent.

At this point, you will gear your teaching toward the habits, processes, and qualities of good writing that independent writers possess. Now, more than ever, is the time for you to teach your students to mine their repertoires, understand the power of each genre to communicate a message, find authors that inspire them, and put those pieces together to create the kinds of writing projects that inspire others.

Some children will choose genres you have not taught previously, and you'll find it helpful to gather these students together and teach them a few key strategies for writing in that genre. For instance, if a few kids want to write greeting cards, your tips might be something like, decide what kind of card you want to make (what occasion, for whom), create a message that matches the purpose of the card, and make sure your message is for the person who will get the card. As children do their own writing and study mentors in one genre or another, encourage them to add to the list of tips you've begun for them.

BEND IV: PREPARE FOR PUBLICATION

Teach students to revise with independence. Remind them of revision strategies and tools that they have used throughout the year.

As the unit winds down, children will choose one of their projects to publish. In units past, you might have said to your students, "Today, when you revise, you could change your lead to begin with a description of the weather or with an action," and then, predictably, all of your children may have changed their leads to include just that. Since this unit is about true independence, we suggest that, instead of teaching kids which way you want them to revise their pieces, you teach them to think about what their pieces need to make them the best they can be. Refer your students to your shared classroom charts on ways to elaborate or to craft charts the class created when you studied mentor texts and direct them again to the Information, Opinion, and Narrative Writing Checklists.

Remind children that revision strategies include cutting, stapling, adding into the middle of a page, and resequencing. Of course, you want them to know not only the physical work of revision but also the reasons for altering a draft. Remind them that writers put their work into the world for other people to read, so they want to make sure that it's clear to readers, that it says what they want it to say, and that it jumps off the page for readers, making them laugh, smile, nod in agreement, or sigh.

Certainly, you will want to nudge children to add more to both their pictures and their words. A child who has written about jumping waves with her dad might notice that she can say more about how the sun sparkled on the water or about seagulls flying overhead in a *V* formation. In addition, children can add actions. They can think about exactly what their bodies were doing (in stories) or what they imagine them doing (in poems)—maybe their arms are flapping or their feet are tapping or they were curled up in a ball—and what the people or animals were doing too. For example, in *Sheila Rae's Peppermint Stick* by Kevin Henkes, Sheila Rae stumbled, the books fell, the stool tipped, and the peppermint stick broke. We really can picture what happened here. This is a nice time to remind children of the envisioning work they do in reading. They picture what is happening when they read, so they need to create a picture for their reader when they write. This is the building block for showing, not telling, through actions.

Adding details is an important part of revision too. Remind children how to reread their pieces thinking about which part is the most important. Often, this will be the very thing that made them want to write their piece in the first place. If kids are having a hard time figuring out the most important part, they might ask themselves, "Where in my story do I have the biggest feelings?" This is the part we want children to stretch out with details that spotlight what makes this moment essential. For example, a child rereading a story he wrote about cooking *arroz con pollo* with *Abuelo* on Saturday might realize that the most important part happened when he and his *abuelo* smelled something burning. This might be the part of the story he will want to develop further, adding in dialogue and small actions.

You may also want to remind children that they can add new beginnings or endings. Show them that they can try writing a few different beginnings or endings and then think about which one works best. One way to have kids try out new beginnings and endings is to study some mentor texts. Being able to name what the writer did in his or her beginning or ending can be a useful step for young writers who are working on their own beginnings and endings.

Have students revise by rereading, both as a writer and as a reader.

Above all, encourage children to reread. They will have already learned the importance of this, and now you will have the opportunity to spotlight it again. Remind children to reread not only entire pieces but short sections too, asking themselves if what they've written is clear, if a reader would understand it, if they've written exactly what they intended to say. Tell children to notice both how the writing sounds and how it looks. Are there spaces between words? Punctuation? Do the words look right? Children can work in partnerships, showing each other places they've revised and helping each other plan possible revision strategies. They can act out stories and how-tos together to make sure they can picture what is happening and to find places to add more actions or dialogue or feeling or thinking. Children can read and reread their stories to their partners, using the Narrative Writing Checklist and together think more deeply about their pieces.

You might also encourage children to picture their readers reading their pieces when they are all finished. Do they envision a reader laughing? Feeling scared? Likely, children will find places they need to revise to achieve that effect. Again, children might want to draw on the mentor texts they have been using to see how those writers make the piece scary or funny, for example, and use what they notice to add to their own writing. They could also read their pieces aloud to partners to see what kind of reactions they get.

Rally students to edit, add final touches, and prepare for publication.

Children will then edit their pieces by themselves and with a partner in ways that match the Common Core State Standards' expectations for second-graders. They will respond to questions and suggestions from their peers and will check to be sure they have written with punctuation, spelled words as correctly as they can, and reread their writing often, making sure it looks right, makes sense, and sounds right. This is also a good time to make sure that kids are using any editing checklists that you have developed together in other units. Be sure that the expectations on the editing checklists are aligned to the CCSS. One way to ensure this is to use the "Language Conventions" section of the writing checklists.

When it comes time to make finishing touches, children can think about all the ways they have polished their writing so far this year and decide which ways will work best for this new project. Do they want to add a dedication and an "about the author" page? Do they want to create a blurb on the back of the book? Do they want to use different materials from the art center to make the covers of their books? Mentor texts will also serve as great sources of inspiration.

As the unit winds down, you'll want to make choices about the kind of class celebration you and your children will hold. The kinds of texts they create will certainly play a role in this decision, and a museum of writing is often a great way to display a variety of writing genres. In this instance, children will display drafts, mentor texts, and published pieces for visitors. As these visitors tour the museum, children can discuss the reasons for their choices in both genre and publication. After the museum, once the guests have bid farewell, children might take a quiet moment to reflect on what they learned about themselves as writers in this unit and make goals for themselves for over the summer. Or, after visiting a neighborhood bookstore, the children might set up the classroom to resemble a bookstore with separate sections for each genre, posters advertising "Meet the Author" events, and an area for author readings. You can record these readings and put them up on a class website. Some schools have scanned the children's books and then displayed them on a virtual bookshelf.

Part Two: Differentiating Instruction for Individuals and Small Groups: If . . . Then . . . Conferring Scenarios

MASTERING THE ART OF CONFERRING PROVES to be many teachers' greatest endeavor. Even if you believe in it and read endlessly about it, when the reality of writing workshop sets in, you may often feel inadequate and unprepared. All of us have our stories. I remember Alexandra, tall with long brown hair and a thick Russian accent. I'd pull up beside her after the minilesson, notebook in hand, ready to execute the perfect conference. We'd talk, I'd research, and without fail, every time, I'd be left with the same terrifying realization: "She's already doing everything! I don't know what to teach her." In an attempt to preserve my own integrity, I'd leave her with a compliment. Despite having joined our class mid-year, despite the challenge of mastering a new language and adapting to a new culture, Alexandra implemented anything and everything I hoped she would as a writer. I thought, what should she do next? I was stuck.

Then there was a child I'll call Matthew, who in truth, represents many others across my years as a teacher. It felt as if I was always conferring with him—modeling, pulling him into small groups, implementing all the scaffolds I knew of—and yet he didn't make the progress I hoped for. In reality, it felt like nothing worked. As I'd sit beside him, looking over his work, I couldn't help but wonder what was happening. Why was my teaching passing him over? What do I teach him, right now in this conference, when his writing needs *everything*?

We've all had Alexandras and Matthews, as well as the children who fall somewhere in the gray areas between. And conferring with these children is a challenging, nuanced art that we all seek to master. Many of us ask the same questions: "What do I teach this child? How do I help him?"

Visiting hundreds of schools gives you a unique perspective, one that is difficult to see when you are in one classroom, with one set of children with very particular needs. You begin to see patterns. You begin to notice that when X is taught, children often need Y or Z. You meet an Alexandra in Chicago and another in Tulsa, Oklahoma. You meet Matthews in Seattle and Shanghai. And you begin to realize that, despite the uniqueness of each child, there are particular ways they struggle and predictable ways you can help. We can use all we know about child development, learning progressions, writing craft, and grade-specific standards to anticipate and plan for the individualized instruction our students are apt to need.

These charts are designed to do just that. We've anticipated the most common struggles you will see as you teach narrative, opinion, and informational writing through the units of study and have named a bit about these in the "If . . ." column of this chart. When you identify a child (or a group of children) in need of work in that particular area, gather them together for a conference or small group. Then, teach them the strategy named in the column titled "After acknowledging what the child is doing well, you might say . . ." We've laid out not only the specific strategy you might teach, but the way you might contextualize the work for your writers. Of course, you should feel free to use your own language and change this section accordingly. What we've presented is just one way your teaching might go!

Finally, plan to leave the writer with a tangible artifact of your work together. This will ensure that he or she remembers the strategy you've worked on and will allow you to look back and see what you taught the last time you met. It will be important for you to follow up on the goals you leave children with. Plan to check in a few days post-conference with a quick, "How has the work we talked about been going for you? Can you show me where you've tried it?"

Many teachers choose to print the "Leave the writer with . . . " column onto stickers (so they can be easily placed in students' notebooks). You also might choose to print them out on plain paper (see the CD-ROM for these charts in reproducible form) and tape them in the writer's notebook or onto the writer's desk as a reminder. You'll notice that we've tried to name the strategy in a way that has a chartlike quality, so that students can look back and be reminded of what they are working on.

We hope these charts will help you to anticipate, spot, and teach into the challenges your writers face during the independent work portion of your writing workshop.

Narrative Writing

If ...	After acknowledging what the child is doing well, you might say ...	Leave the writer with ...
Structure and Cohesion		
The story lacks focus. This writer has written a version of a "bed to bed" story, beginning with the start of a day or large event ("I woke up and had breakfast.") and progressing to the end ("I came home. It was a great day."). The event unfolds in a bit-by-bit fashion, with each part of the story receiving equal weight.	You are learning to write more and more, stretching your stories across tons of pages. That's great. But here's the new challenge. Writers need to be able to write a lot and still write a *focused* story. What I mean by this is that writers can write a whole story that only lasts 20 minutes, and it can still be tons of pages long. To write a really fleshed out, well developed Small Moment story, it is important to move more slowly through the sequence of the event, and capture the details on the page.	Not the whole trip, the whole day: 20 minutes!! Write with details I said, I thought, I did. Write with details! I said I thought I did Not the whole day! 20 minutes!
The story is confusing or seems to be missing important information. This writer has written a story that leaves you lost, unable to picture the moment or understand the full sequence of events. She may have left out information regarding where she was or why something was happening, or may have switched suddenly to a new part of the story without alerting the reader.	I really want to understand this story, but it gets confusing for me. Will you remember that writers need to become readers and to reread their own writing, asking, "Does this make sense? Have I left anything out that my reader might need to know?" Sometimes it is helpful to ask a partner to read your story, as well, and to tell you when the story is making sense (thumbs up) and when it is confusing (thumbs down).	I reread my writing to make it more clear. I ask myself, "Does this make sense? Have I left anything out that my reader might need to know?" If I need to, I add more information or a part that is missing into the story.

If …	After acknowledging what the child is doing well, you might say …	Leave the writer with …
The story has no tension. This writer's story is flat, without any sense of conflict or tension. The story is more of a chronicle than a story. If there is a problem, there is no build up around possible solutions. Instead, the dog is simply lost and then found.	You told what happened in your story, in order, so I get it. But to make this into the kind of story that readers can't put down, the kind that readers read by flashlight in bed, you have to add what writers call edge-of-the-seat tension. Instead of just saying I did this, I did this, I did this, you need to have the narrator want something really badly and then run into difficulties, or trouble … so readers are thinking, "Will it work? Won't it?" You got to get readers all wound up! Right now, reread and find the part of the story where you could show what the main character really wants.	Edge-of-the-seat tension: 1. someone who really wants something. 2. someone encounters trouble. 3. someone tries, tries, tries. 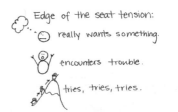
The writer is new to the writing workshop or this particular genre of writing. This writer struggles because narrative is a new genre for her. She may display certain skill sets (e.g., the ability to use beautifully descriptive language or literary devices) but lacks the vision of what she is being asked to produce. Her story is probably long and unfocused and is usually dominated by summary, not storytelling.	Someone famously once said, "You can't hit a target if you don't know what that target is." This is especially true for writers. They can't write well if they don't have a vision, a mental picture, of what they hope to produce. Today, I want to teach you that one way writers learn about the kinds of writing they hope to produce is by studying mentor texts. They read a mentor text once, enjoying it as a story. Then, they read it again, this time asking, "How does this kind of story seem to go?" They label what they notice and then try it in their own writing.	Writers use mentor texts to help them imagine what they hope to write. They: • Read the text and enjoy it as a good story. • Reread the text and ask, "How does this kind of story seem to go?" • Note what they notice. • Try to do some of what they noticed in their own writing.

Elaboration

The writer has created a story that is sparse, with little elaboration. This writer has written a story that is short, with one or more parts that need elaboration. He has conveyed the main outline of an event (this happened, then this happened, then this happened), but there is no sense that he has expanded on any one particular part.	You have gotten skilled at telling what happens, in order, but you write with just the bare bones sequence. Like, if you went out for supper yesterday and I asked you, "How was your dinner at the restaurant?" And you answered, "I went to the restaurant. I ate food. It was good," that's not the best story, right? It is just the bare bones with no flesh on them—like a skeleton. Can you try to flesh your story out?	Not: I ate food. I came home. But: Details, details, details. or: Not

If . . .	After acknowledging what the child is doing well, you might say . . .	Leave the writer with . . .
The writer seems to throw in a lot of random details. This writer adds details that probably aren't anything that the narrator would have noticed. ("I took the green dollar bill and put it in my right back pocket.")	This is going to sound like funny advice—but here it is. Writers write with *honest* details. By honest, I don't just mean that writers put in the true details: "I ate 26 strands of spaghetti." That could be true, but I don't think anyone, eating a nice bowl of spaghetti, would honestly notice how many strands they ate. But this might be an honest detail: "I ate a big bowl of spaghetti. My mom kept glancing over at me like she was mad. I think maybe I was making those slurping noises that she says are so rude. I tried to slurp really quietly." Whatever you are writing about, try to remember what you truly did notice, what you honestly paid attention to, and add those details.	A Goal: HONEST details: Not 26 strands of spaghetti . . . but tried to slurp quietly.
The story is swamped with dialogue. This writer is attempting to story-tell, not summarize, but is relying too heavily on dialogue to accomplish this mission. The story is full of endless dialogue ("Let's play at the park," I said. "Okay," Jill said. "Maybe we should play on the swings," I said. "I agree," Jill said. "Great!" I said.). This writer needs to learn that dialogue is an important part of storytelling but cannot be the only device a writer uses to move a story forward.	Sometimes, writers make their characters talk—and talk and talk and talk. Today, I want to teach you that writers use dialogue, but they use it sparingly. They make sure their writing has a balance of action and dialogue by alternating between the two and by cutting dialogue that does not give the reader important information about the character or the story.	Writers make sure that their writing has a balance of dialogue and action: • They often alternate between action and dialogue as they write. • They cut dialogue that does not give the reader important information about the character or story. Dialogue AND action Cut dialogue that is not important!
The writer does what you teach, that day. This writer doesn't seem to draw on a full repertoire of strategies. As a result, the writer's texts tend to display one aspect of good writing, and not others.	Can you imagine if I taught you to ride a bike, and on day one, I taught you to pedal, and on day two, I taught you to hang on, and day three, to balance, and day four, to stop . . . and you only did what I taught you that day? So day one, you only pedaled all day. And day four, you only stopped all day. How do you think that would go? You are right—it would be kind of awful, right, because to ride a bike, you have to do all those things. Well, I'm telling you this because I feel like when I teach you stuff about good stories, you do what I taught you on that day, but you don't remember to do stuff from other days. Like if one day I taught you to make your characters talk, and the next day I taught you that it helps to bring out the setting in your story, on the second day, I'm hoping you will do BOTH—make your characters talk and also bring out the setting. One thing that would really help you, I think, is for you to reread our class charts more often, and think, "Did I remember to do that in this piece?"	The anchor chart, turned into an individual checklist.

If ...	After acknowledging what the child is doing well, you might say ...	Leave the writer with ...
Language		
The writer summarizes rather than story-tells. There is probably a sense that this writer is disconnected from the series of events—listing what happened first, then next, then next. He writes predominately by overviewing what happened ("On the way to school I was almost attacked by a dog but I got there okay."). The writer rarely uses dialogue, descriptive details, or other forms of narrative craft to convey the story to his reader.	Writers don't take huge steps through their experience, writing like this "I had an argument. Then I went to bed." Instead, writers take tiny steps, writing more like this, "'It was your turn!' I yelled and then I turned and walked out of the room really fast. I slammed the door and went to my bedroom. I was so furious that I just sat on my bed for a long time." It helps to show what happened rather than just telling the main gist of it.	Not giant steps, but baby steps. Show, not tell. Not giant steps Baby steps!
The writer struggles with spelling. This writer's piece is riddled with spelling mistakes. This does not necessarily mean the writing is not strong (in fact, the story may be very strong), but the spelling mistakes compromise the reader's ability to understand it. The writer's struggle with spelling may stem from various places—difficulty understanding and applying spelling patterns, a limited stock of high-frequency words, lack of investment, the acquisition of English as a new language—and diagnosing the underlying problem will be an important precursor to teaching into it.	One of the things I'm noticing about your writing is how beautiful it sounds when you read it aloud. I looked more closely, curious about how I had missed all the beauty you've captured on this page, and realized that all your spelling mistakes make it difficult for me (and probably other readers, too) to understand. Today, I want to teach you a few techniques writers use to help them spell. Writers use the classroom word wall, they stretch words out and write down the sounds they hear, and they use words they *do* know how to spell to help them with those they *don't* know how to spell.	Writers work hard at their spelling. They: • Use the **word wall** • **S-T-R-E-T-C-H** words out and write down the sounds they hear • Use words they **know** (*found*), to help them spell words they **don't know** (*compound*, *round*)
The writer does not use end punctuation when she writes. This writer tends to write without using end punctuation. She may pause after a sentence and forget to write the mark, or she may connect her sentences with a conjunction such as *and*. This writer tends not to reread her sentences, pages, or piece to see if what she wrote makes sense and to see if she has used end punctuation.	You are forgetting that writers use punctuation at the end of sentences—like street signs—to tell readers when to stop and take a breath as they are reading. The punctuation signals that the idea is done and a new one is coming. One thing that you can do to remind yourself to write with punctuation is that once you get to the end of a part of your writing, you should reread your writing. As you reread, listen to when your voice takes a break and think, "What should I use here? A question mark, an exclamation point, or a period?"	Did I remember to use punctuation? . Period ! Exclamation Point ? Question Mark

If ...	After acknowledging what the child is doing well, you might say ...	Leave the writer with ...
The writer struggles with end punctuation. This story amounts to what appears to be one long, endless sentence. The writer may have distinct sentences ("We ran down the road James was chasing us we thought we needed to run faster to escape him") that are simply not punctuated. Alternatively, he may have strung his sentences together using an endless number of *ands*, *thens*, and *buts* in an attempt at cohesion. ("We ran down the road and James was chasing us and we thought that we needed to run faster to escape him but then we could hear his footsteps and his breathing and we were scared.")	I read your piece today, and it sounded a bit like this. "We ran down the road and James was chasing us and we thought that we needed to run faster to escape him but then we could hear his footsteps and his breathing and we were scared." Phew, I was out of breath! Today, I want to teach you that writers use end punctuation to give their readers a little break, to let them take a breath, before moving onto the next thing that happened in the story. One way to figure out where to put end punctuation is to reread your piece aloud, notice where you find yourself stopping to take a small breath, and put a period, exclamation point, or question mark there.	Writers reread their pieces aloud, notice where readers should stop and take a small breath because one thought has ended, and use end punctuation to help mark those places.
The writer has capital letters scattered throughout sentences, not just at the beginnings of them. This writer tends to have capital letters in the middle of words and in the middle of sentences. She may not know all of her lowercase letters, or she may know them but be more comfortable using uppercase letters. In general, though, this writer tends not to care whether she switches between lower and uppercase letters.	You know, one time I went to a restaurant for a nice dinner. I got there, and I realized I had forgotten my shoes!!!! I had to walk into the restaurant without any shoes on. I'm telling you this because when you write, you aren't forgetting your shoes ... but you do something sort of like that. Do you know what you do? You actually use capital letters in the middles of your sentences for no reason at all! When people saw me walk into that restaurant with just my socks on, they probably thought, "Huh?" and I bet they are thinking the same thing when they see capital letters in the middles of words in your writing. I think you are old enough to decide that writing capitals for no reason is the old way, and now you are doing the new way. From now on, remember that writers use capital letters at the beginnings of sentences, for names of people, and for the word *I*. After you write a page, you will probably want to reread it to check your capitals. You can be like a detective and search your whole writing to find "capitals that are mess ups." If it helps, keep an alphabet chart next to you that has both uppercase and lowercase letters. This can help you remember how to make the lowercase letters if you forget.	An alphabet chart with lower and uppercase letters

If …	After acknowledging what the child is doing well, you might say …	Leave the writer with …
The Process of Generating Ideas		
The writer struggles with thinking about an idea for a story. This writer often sits for long periods of time contemplating what to write. He tends not to have many pieces. This may be because he does not use a strategy to help himself, or it may be that he does not think the things in his life are worth writing about, or he may have distractions that prevent him from self-initiating.	One thing that you can do as a writer is make a list of possible ideas for stories. You can use our chart, ways to come up with ideas for stories, to help you think of all the many things you have in your life to write about! Then you can pick one and write it. When you are done, you come back to the list and pick another!	Story Ideas 1. _____ 2. _____ 3. _____ 4. _____ 5. _____
The writer returns to the same story repeatedly. This writer has many pieces about the same event. For example, the writer may have three stories, all about biking in the park.	It is nice to write a couple of stories about the same thing—like Cynthia Rylant has a couple of stories about Henry and Mudge, right? And you have a couple of stories about the park. So you are sort of like Cynthia Rylant. But one thing about Cynthia Rylant is she doesn't have Mudge get lost in this story AND in this one AND in this one. He gets lost in one story, he is in a dog show in another story, and he gets in trouble in another story. After this, if one story tells about you bike riding in the park, what could the next story tell about? What else do you do in the park? Great. So, you and Cynthia Rylant are going to be a lot alike, because each of your books will tell about something different.	Stories in the Park 1. bike riding 2. finding a baby bird 3. ?? Stories in the park: 1. 2. 3. To Come Up with a Story Idea, Think of: • Things I like to do • Places I go • People I enjoy spending time with Story Ideas • Things • Places • People

If ...	After acknowledging what the child is doing well, you might say ...	Leave the writer with ...
The Process of Drafting		
The writer has trouble maintaining stamina and volume. This writer has a hard time putting words down on the page. It may be that he writes for a long period of time producing very little or that he refuses to write for longer than a few minutes. The writer often has avoidance behaviors (e.g., trips to the bathroom during writing workshop, a pencil tip that breaks repeatedly). He gets very little writing done during the workshop, despite urging from you.	Today, I want to teach you a little trick that often works for me when I'm having trouble staying focused. When writing is hard for me, I set small, manageable goals for myself. I make sure these goals are something I *know* I can do, like writing for ten minutes straight. Then, when I reach my goal, I give myself a little gift, like a short walk or a few minutes to sketch a picture. Then, I get back to writing again.	Writers set goals for themselves and work hard to achieve them. When they do, they reward themselves for their hard work.
The writer starts many new pieces but just gives up on them halfway through. When you tour the writer's folder you see many pieces that are unfinished. This may be because the writer abandons the piece to start a new one or it may be because the writer does not get a chance to finish the piece on day one, and on day two the writer does not look back in her folder to decide what to work on. Rather, she starts a new piece each day.	Each day in the workshop you have a decision to make: to work on a piece on the green-dot side, pieces that are not finished yet, or start a new piece. When I look at your folder, I see you have many pieces that are on the green-dot side that are not finished! That's so sad ... all those unfinished stories. How awful. Don't you think those stories deserve to be finished? After this, why don't you look through the green-dot side of your folder and see if there is a story that isn't finished. That story is probably calling to you, saying "Finish me!" So—hear the stories call, okay, and reread it. Then think, "What happens next? What else was happening in this story? How does it end?" When you have written the ending, you can reread and revise it like always. Then you can put it on the red-dot side.	A "Reread me first!" sign on the green dot side of the folder. Ask : What happens next? How does this story end?

If …	After acknowledging what the child is doing well, you might say …	Leave the writer with …
The writer tends to write short pieces with few words or sentences. This writer may have several pieces in her folder, but she has few words or sentences written in each story. It seems as though the writer may not spend a great deal of time on a piece. She may write a couple of pieces in one sitting. This writer tends not to reread her pieces or try to push herself to say and write more on the page.	What I am noticing about your stories is that they tend to look like this (I make a quick page with a sparse drawing and a single squiggle for a line of print). But I think you, as a writer, are ready to make stories more like this (and I make a quick page with a much more full drawing, and 5 lines of squiggles, representing print). What do you need to go from this (I point to the first drawing) to this (I point to the second drawing)? Right now, will you try a new story and make it more like this? (the second way) Show me how you get ready to write. Okay, will you do that again, but this time when you touch and tell the story on each page, will you touch the top of the writing and say what you will write first and then touch the middle of the writing and say what you will write next and then touch the bottom of the writing—on that page—and say what you will write last. Like this: I put the worm on the hook. (I touched the top of the page.) Now, instead of jumping to the next page—where I catch a fish, I'll say more. I got worm gook on my fingers. (I touch the middle of the page.) It was disgusting, the worm kept wiggling. (I touch the bottom of the page.) Now I can go to the next page.	A Post-it with "Write long and strong." or "More, more, more!" written on it. (As you leave the Post-it, remind the student to use the classroom chart to help her remember ways to add more to her writing.) 
The writer's folder lacks volume of pieces. This writer tends to have very few pieces in his folder, maybe one or two. He tends to go back to the same piece each day and add more. Usually, the additions are sparse, maybe a word or two. Perhaps the writer is spending more time adding to the drawing.	Last night at home, I was looking for your work … and I looked (I imitated looking and finding little) and I looked (I looked under the folder, around it) and I looked!! And I hardly found any work. What do you think has gotten in the way of you getting a lot of work done? Child: I get stuck a lot. Well, after this, when you get stuck, you are going to have to get help so you get unstuck—and fast! Because you need to get a LOT of writing done. Let's make a plan. Today, I am pretty sure you can fill these pages of your book, so I am going to write "Monday" on these pages. Tomorrow, what do you think you can get done if you don't let yourself get stuck? So let's label those pages "Tuesday." Now … you have a lot to do. So will you remember, touch the pages and say aloud what you are going to write, then come back and write it. And if you get stuck, ask for help. Come get me. Because you HAVE to meet these deadlines.	Have I added all that I can? 1. Reread and ask yourself, "Did I add all I can add?" 2. Check with a tool: an exemplar, book, or chart. 3. Add more if you can. 4. When you have tried all you can, start a new piece.  The notes "Monday" and "Tuesday" suffice as a deadline.

If ...	After acknowledging what the child is doing well, you might say ...	Leave the writer with ...
The writer struggles to work independently. This student is often at your side, asking questions or needing advice. She struggles to write on her own and only seems to generate ideas when you are sitting beside her. When she does write, she needs constant "checks" and accolades. She is task-oriented. That is, she will complete one thing you have taught her to do and then sit and wait to be told what to do next. She does not rely on charts or other materials to keep her going.	As a writer, it is important that you take control of your own writing life. You can't be content to sit back and relax. Instead, you have to ask yourself, "What in this room might help me get back on track as a writer?" Then, you use those resources to get started again. You can look at charts in the room, ask your partner for help, read mentor texts for inspiration, or even look back over old writing for new ideas. or One thing I'm noticing about you as a writer is that you write with me in mind. What I mean by this is that when I teach something, you try it. When I suggest something, you try it. But I am not the only writing teacher in this room. Believe it or not, *you* can be your own writing teacher, too. Today, I want to teach you how to look at your own work against a checklist, assess for what is going well and what you might do better, and then set goals for how you might revise your current piece and for what you might try out in your future work, too.	When you are stuck, you can: • Consult charts • Ask your partner for help • Read mentor texts for inspiration • Look back over old writing for new ideas

The Process of Revision

The writer rarely adds to the writing without prompting and support. When asked, "How do you know that you are done?" the writer tends to say she is done because she is on the last page. She tends not to reread her writing to consider adding more or revising. When prompted or reminded to reread and think about what she can add, the writer is willing to think and add more to her writing.	One thing writers do, when they finish their last page, is they reread the whole book and think, "What else can I say? What else happened in this story?" They turn back to page 1 and use their pictures to help them imagine more and use the movie in their mind to capture more details on the page.	Revise: Make a movie in your mind.

If ...	After acknowledging what the child is doing well, you might say ...	Leave the writer with ...
The writer usually adds to his writing rather than takes things away. This writer tends to elaborate on each page of his writing, usually adding in more details about what he did and said and how he felt. He rarely takes out parts or information that do not belong, relate, or make sense to the story.	When writers revise, they don't only add more to help show what is happening and how they feel. They *also* take things out that don't belong or make sense in their story. One thing you can do as a writer is to revise and take things out that don't belong. One way to do this is to reread and ask yourself, "Does this belong in my story? Does it make sense?"	Revise: 1. Does it belong in my story? 2. If no, X it out. Revise: • + add information • − take out information
The writer tends to revise by elaborating, rather than narrowing and finding the focus of the piece. This writer tends to revise only by elaborating on the story. She does not think about revising the structure or focus of her piece. She is not the type of writer who tears off pages to find the important part of her story to say more about it. She tends to add more to each part, regardless of the focus.	Writers revise by adding more. They also revise by thinking about showing the important part of their story. They think, "What do I really want to show and tell my reader?" And they revise accordingly. One thing that you can do before you try to add on to your pieces is ask yourself, "What is the most important part of my story?" One thing writers do is take off the pages that aren't about that part and add more pages to tell about that important part. They try to add their details about the important part of the story.	**The writer tends to revise by elaborating, rather than narrowing and finding the focus of the piece.** This writer tends to revise only by elaborating on the story. She does not think about revising the structure or focus of her piece. She is not the type of writer who tears off pages to find the important part of her story to say more about it. She tends to add more to each part, regardless of the focus.
The writer does not seem to be driven by personal goals so much as by your instructions. If you ask, "What are you working on?" this writer acts surprised. "My writing," she says, and indeed, you are pretty sure that is what she is doing. She is trying to crank out the required amount of text. She doesn't have more specific goals about how to do things better that are influencing her.	Can I ask you something? Who is the boss of your writing? I'm asking that because you need to be the boss of your writing, and to be the best boss you can be, you need to give yourself little assignments. You need to take yourself by the hand and say, "From now on, you should be working on this," and then after a bit, "Now you should be working on this."	My Writing Goals Are: _____ _____ _____

If ...	After acknowledging what the child is doing well, you might say ...	Leave the writer with ...
The Process of Editing		
The writer does not use what she knows to edit her piece. When this writer is rereading her work, she edits very few things. When you prompt the writer or remind her to edit and fix up her writing, she is able to do so.	One thing that writers do when they have revised their stories as best they can is that they reread their pieces and edit their mistakes. They fix their spelling and their punctuation the best they can. One way to do this is to reread your story carefully, from start to finish, a couple of times. You might first reread it to make sure that there aren't any missing words and fix up any easy errors that stand out, like end punctuation you missed or spelling that you wrote too quickly.	Reread and Edit • Find missing words • Fix spelling • Check punctuation
The writer does not use what he knows about editing while writing. This writer is not applying what he knows about spelling, grammar, and punctuation while writing. You may notice that you have taught a particular spelling pattern, he mastered it in isolation, but he is not using that knowledge during writing workshop. He may also spell word wall words wrong or misspell words that are similar (e.g., spelling *getting* correctly but misspelling *setting*). This writer needs to be reminded that editing is not something left for the last stages of writing. Instead, writers use all they know *as they write*.	You are the boss of your own writing, and part of being the boss is making sure that you are doing, and using, everything you know while you write. Often when people think of editing, they think of it as something they do just before publishing. This is true, but it is also true that writers edit as they write. Today, I want to teach you that writers use an editing checklist to remind them of what they've learned about spelling, punctuation, and grammar. They take a bit of time each day to make sure they are using all they know as they write.	Editing Checklist • Read, asking, "Will this make sense to a stranger?" • Check the punctuation. • Do your words look like they are spelled correctly?
The writer does not know what in her piece needs editing. The writer, while editing, may skip over many words and miss many opportunities to fix punctuation. She is unable to find many of the errors she has made. She is not always sure what she is looking for and therefore may be overwhelmed.	Sometimes when you are editing, there may be times when you feel like you can't find any errors! That's when you really have to challenge yourself. One thing that you might do as a writer is to choose a couple of words to think more about—ones that you aren't sure if they are spelled correctly. You can choose them and think, "Are there other ways to spell this word? How else could it look? Is there another way to make some of these sounds?" You might try the word a few different ways to see if you can find a better spelling.	Try Your Spelling a Few Times: 1. _____ 2. _____ 3. _____

Information Writing

If …	After acknowledging what the child is doing well, you might say …	Leave the writer with …
Structure and Cohesion		
The writer is new to this particular genre. This writer may actually write in another genre. Instead of writing an information book about her topic ("All About Dogs"), she may end up writing a narrative about her topic ("One day I took my dog for a walk").	You've got a nice start to a story here. You are telling one thing that happened—you took your dog for a walk. But actually, right now we are writing all-about pieces. The pieces we are writing now aren't stories, they are all-about nonfiction books that teach people true stuff about a topic. One thing that you want to do as a writer is to teach your reader the information about the topic, rather than tell them a story about one time when something happened to you. To do this, one thing you might do is name the topic and the information that you can teach your reader. Say the list across your fingers, and then you can draw and write it across pages.	Teaching Book: • Name a topic • Teach information (You may leave the writer a couple of nonfiction books from the leveled library to help her remember what an information book is.) *Teaching Book:* *Name a topic.* *Teach information*

If …	After acknowledging what the child is doing well, you might say …	Leave the writer with …
The writer has not established a clear organization for his book. This writer is struggling with organization. It is likely that his book is a jumble of information about a larger topic, with no clear subheadings or internal organization. The writer may have a table of contents but the chapters actually contain a whole bunch of stuff unrelated to the chapter titles or the writer may have skipped this part of the process all together.	One of the most important things information writers do is organize their writing. Making chapters or headings is one way to make it easier for your readers learn about your topic. It's like creating little signs that say, "Hey, reader, I'm about to start talking about a new part of my topic!" It helps to name what the upcoming part of your writing will be about and then to write about just that thing. When information writers notice they are about to start writing about something new, they often create a new heading that tells the reader what the next part will be about.	<u>One thing</u> About that thing About that thing About that thing <u>Another thing</u> About that next thing About that next thing ~~Something else~~ ~~Something else~~ <u>Another thing</u> <u>Not:</u> One thing Another thing The first thing A whole other thing
The writer does not have a clear beginning and/or ending to her text. This writer tends to start (and possibly end as well) her books with an information page that seems as if it is just randomly chosen.	I want to ask you to do something. Pretend the phone is ringing, and lift up the receiver, okay? "Ring ring." The child says: "Hello?" "And then he stopped seeing his patients. He just wrote them letters and said he was too old to be their Goodbye." I stopped. How would that be as a phone conversation? Pretty weird, right? I agree. It would be weird because there wasn't any start to it, or any finish. There was no introduction, no overview, and there was no closing. I am telling you this because your writing seems to go like that a lot. Your book just starts in teaching something about your topic. There isn't any place where you talk to the reader and you tell the reader what the whole book will be about and why you have written it, that sort of thing. Do you want to study the way other people start books and see if you want to begin starting your books in a more usual way? If you decide to change the way you start books so it is more usual, who knows, you might end up thinking about the way you end books as well. * * * One thing that writers do to end their information book is they think about the topic and why it is important to know and learn about. Sometimes writers tell their readers what they hope for in the future.	Starts and Endings: • What am I writing about? • Why is this important? • What do I hope you learn, think, feel?

If …	After acknowledging what the child is doing well, you might say …	Leave the writer with …
Information is overlapping in various sections. This writer attempted to organize his piece, but has various sections that overlap. The writer may have repeated similar information in several parts of his piece or may have attempted to give the same information worded differently. Often he has sections and subsections that are too closely related and therefore struggles to find different information for different parts.	It is great that you have a system for organizing things. It is sort of like this page is a drawer and you just put things about (XYZ) in it. And this chapter is a drawer and you just put stuff about (ABC) in it. There are a few mess ups—places where you have some whole other things scattered in, or some things that are in two places. That always happens. You got to expect it. So what writers do is just what you have done. They write organized pieces. But then, when they are done writing, they … Do you know? They reread to check. Just like you can reread to check your spelling, you can reread to check that the right things are in the right drawers, the right sections.	Writers reread to check that things are in the right drawers.
The writer has included facts as she thinks about them. This writer tends to write without planning. She starts writing any information that comes to mind and in any order. The result is a text with information that is not grouped together on a page or in a chapter.	You know what I think is happening? You have so much to say that when you pick up your pen, you just start writing right away, without thinking, "Wait. How will my book go?" I'm glad you have a lot to teach, but now that you are getting to be almost six years old, I think you are old enough to do what professional writers do—the people who write the books in our library. When they sit down to write a book, instead of just starting by writing one thing that comes to mind, they say, "Wait a minute. How will my whole book go?" and then they plan out what they will write about on one page, and on another page. Are you willing to try that planning while I am here to help? Yes?! Great. And after this, whenever you go to write a book, remember to do like the pros and to say, "Wait. How will my whole book go?" Then you can plan by making a Table of Contents, or by sketching what goes on each page.	WAIT! How will my whole book go? 1. Table of Contents 2. Pictures

Elaboration		
The writer provides information in vague or broad ways. This writer's books are list-like, with broad terms and few supporting details. "Dogs play. Dogs eat. Dogs sleep."	When you are teaching information, it is important to teach your reader lots of information—on every page, you teach the reader some information. One way that writers think up details to teach is by thinking, "What would readers want to know about my topic? What questions would they ask?" Then writers answer those questions.	Page 1: information Page 2: information Page 3: Information **Ask and Answer Questions** • Why? • When? • How?
Each section is short and needs to be elaborated upon. This writer has attempted to group her information, but each section is short. For example, she may have listed one or two facts related to a specific subsection but is stuck for what to add next.	Information writers need to be able to say a lot about each part of their topic, or to elaborate. There are a few things you can do to make each part of your book chock-full of information. One thing that helps is to write in partner sentences. This means that instead of writing one sentence about each thing, you can push yourself to write two sentences (or more) about each thing. So if I said, "George sits at a desk when he is at school" and I wanted to write with partner sentences, what else might I say about George sitting at his desk? You are right. It can help to fill in stuff about why, kinds of, where, how many, and so on. A whole other thing you can do to get yourself to say more is you can use prompts like, "It's also important to know this because ..."; "Also ..."; and "What this means is ..."	Writers Elaborate 1. They check to make sure they have at least four or five pieces of information for each subtopic. If not, they consider cutting that section and starting a new one. 2. Writers elaborate by creating partner sentences. 3. They use prompts like "It's also important to know ..."; "Also ..."; and "What this means is ..." to say more about a particular piece of information.

If …	After acknowledging what the child is doing well, you might say …	Leave the writer with …
The writer goes off on tangents when elaborating. This writer has tried to elaborate on information but tends to get into personal and tangential details ("Dogs really are great pets. I have a dog, too. I had a cat, too, but she peed on the counter so my Dad got rid of her."). Or by repeating the same information again and again. Or by being chit-chatty ("And I love LOVE that and think it is really funny, so so funny.").	You are working hard to say a lot about your topic, aren't you? I have to give you a tip, though. Sometimes, in your hard work to say a lot, you are doing things that don't really work that well. Let me give you an example of things that don't work when writers are writing information books, and will you see if you do those things some of the time? Pretend I was writing about dogs, so I wrote that there are many kinds of dogs, and the kinds of dogs are divided into groups, like spaniels, retrievers, toy dogs, and so forth. If I then said, "And I have a dog and a cat, too, and the cat's name is Barney … " would that go in my report? You are right. It wouldn't go because it isn't really teaching information and ideas about the topic—and it might not even be about the topic. If I wrote "And I Love Love LOVE dogs," would that go? And if I said, "Some dogs are spaniels, some are retrievers," would that go? You see, there are things people do when they are trying to elaborate, to say more, that just don't work that well. So what writers do is they cross them out and try other ways to elaborate. You will want to reread your writing and to have the courage to say no sometimes. or Today, I want to teach you that information writers revise by checking to make sure all their information is important and new. They cut out parts where they started to talk about their own life too much and got off topic, parts where they included information that doesn't go with what they were writing about, or parts where they repeat the same thing more than once.	Information writers cut parts where: • They started talking about their life too much and got off topic. • They included information that doesn't fit with what the rest of the paragraph is about. • They repeated something they'd already written.

If ...	After acknowledging what the child is doing well, you might say ...	Leave the writer with ...
The writer uses only one way to elaborate in her writing. This writer has one strategy that she overuses to elaborate. For example, she makes comparisons for *every* fact that she writes.	You have gotten really good at comparing, haven't you? You compared here, here, here, here. I am glad you have learned to do that, and you are right that practicing so much has made it so you will always, after this, remember that one way to elaborate on a fact when you are writing an all-about book is to make readers really think about that fact by comparing it to something else. But here is the thing. You are actually doing that one thing—comparing—too much. In fact, you are doing it *way* too much. As you become sort of like a professional writer, you are going to want to go from writing like a kid to writing like a pro. You know how little kids, when they learn to use exclamation points, start using them all the time ... Yeah, they sometimes use whole lines of exclamation points. Well, you are sort of doing the same thing with comparing. You are overusing it. But you are right to want to elaborate, to say more, about a fact before moving on. It's just that the best way to elaborate is to have a little list of different ways you can do that, and then to draw on that whole list of ways. Would you and your partner be willing to work together and start a short list of different ways to elaborate, and then we'll share this list with the rest of the class and get their ideas, too.	A mini-chart from the classroom to help her remember and think about how she can say more in her writing. You may decide to leave the writer with a Post-it that says, "How else can I describe or teach about my information?" You will want to tell the writer to use the chart in the classroom.
The writer writes with lots of good information but it is in helter-skelter order. This writer may have written about two, three, or even four different topics in one book. Or, he may not know how to organize his information.	You know what, your writing hops back and forth from one topic to another to the first again ... like it is about bears, then dogs, then bears again, then dogs, then rabbits, then bears ... it is sort of *crazy*! Usually what a writer does is she puts all the pages that are about one thing together, with a title, and all the pages about something different together, with a title. Maybe you want to use jaws (the staple remover) to take your book apart and see if it can get divided into three books. And another time, when you are writing a book and you think of a whole different topic to write about—get another book. Don't smush it all together in one.	(One topic) (one topic) (one topic)

If …	After acknowledging what the child is doing well, you might say …	Leave the writer with …
The writer invents or makes up information about the topic to elaborate. This writer may invent facts. Usually this information is made-up. It is not rooted in personal experience or any sort of research from books or photographs or other artifacts.	When writers write fiction stories, they make up stuff that isn't true. But you are writing NON-fiction now, or true books. After you write a book, you can reread it and think, "Is this all true?" And if some of it isn't true, then you take it out.	Reread: • True information? or • NOT true?
Language		
The writer does not use a variety of end punctuation in her text. When you read this writer's texts, you see that she mostly uses periods as end punctuation. She may sometimes use a question mark and rarely an exclamation point. She has not reread her writing or considered what end punctuation is needed for each sentence she writes.	As you are writing, will you think more about how you are using end punctuation to talk to your readers? Reread your writing and think which end punctuation you need. You are tending to use only periods, and actually you could be using exclamation points and question marks as well.	Reread and Edit for Punctuation: . Period ! Exclamation Point ? Question Mark
The writer does not use all that he knows about letter sounds/vowel patterns to write words. When you read the writer's work you see that he has one or two letter sounds in his labels. You know from your letter name/sound ID assessment that he knows the other letters and sounds that he is not putting onto the page. When you read the writer's work you see that he has a few words misspelled with vowel work that he is working on in word study. From your spelling assessment, for example, you know the writer knows or is working on short vowel patterns. In his work, though, he does not write with short vowel patterns.	When you write, you want to use all that you know about writing words. Using *all* that you know will help you as well as your reader to read back what you have written and taught in your book. One way that you can help make your writing even more readable is to work on getting more sounds in your words. After you put a letter down for your word, keep saying the word slowly. Listen for the next sound. Slide your finger under the letter you wrote as you listen to the next sound. Keep your alphabet chart here to think about what other letters you hear.	You may decide to have your student use his word sorts to help him study his spelling. Remind the writer to take out his sorts to remind him about the features of phonics that he is studying and working on. These could be in an envelope that he keeps in his writing folder if you make him a set.

If …	After acknowledging what the child is doing well, you might say …	Leave the writer with …
The writer does not use domain-specific vocabulary. This writer has not included specialized words that fit with his topic. For example, if he is writing about dogs, he might say, "This is a dog. You need to walk your dog. Dogs need food. Dogs have babies." The writer does not specify what kind of a dog (a Spaniel or a Maltese), the type of food that dogs eat, or what you call baby dogs—puppies.	When you are teaching information in your books, remember that the reader *also* wants to be an expert. Usually experts know really important words that have to do with their topics. As a nonfiction writer you want to use these words and also teach them to your readers, so that they too can be experts. As you are writing, one way that you can do this is to reread and think about the information and ask yourself, "Did I use all the special words that fit with this information? Is there a better word or a more specific word that fits with this topic that I can use?"	A Post-it with a few key words to reread and think about. You may write on the Post-it, "Look for places to use special words. Think about what important words fit with this topic." 

The Process of Generating Ideas

The writer chooses topics about which he has little expertise. This writer may choose polar bears, for example, and then end up with almost nothing to say.	Writers need to ask: 1. Do I care about this topic? (You are already doing this!) 2. Do I know enough to imagine a possible table of contents? If not, they pick a different topic. If you have picked a topic that you care about but you don't know about, you either need to say no, and go to a topic you know better, or you need to do some research. Watching a video tape or reading a book on the topic REALLY help.	When Choosing a Topic, Information Writers Ask: • Do I care about this topic? • Do I know enough to imagine a possible table of contents? If not: give up the topic, or do some research. 

The Process of Drafting

The first draft is not organized. This writer has written a first draft that is disorganized. It may be that there is an underlying organizational structure (e.g., the writer grouped similar information together), but she did not use new pages, section titles, or transitions to let the reader in on this structure. Alternatively, the writer may have simply "written a draft," compiling all the information she collected into one ongoing piece of writing.	One of the most important things information writers do is organize. It can be hard for a reader to learn a lot of new information about, say, sharks. But when a writer organizes the information into sections, then it becomes easier for the reader to take it in. The reader knows that one part will be about sharks' bodies, another will be about what they eat, and another will be about their family life. As a writer, it's important to look at your draft and make sure that you've organized it in a way that will make sense to the reader. This usually means taking all the information or facts about one part of a topic (like sharks' bodies) and putting that together. Then, taking all the information about another topic (like what sharks eat) and putting that together. Then using section headings to make it clear what each part is about.	Information Writers Organize Their Writing! • Divide your topic into sections (you may have already done this while planning). • Put the information about one section together with a heading. • Put the information about another section together with a heading. • And so on … (Sometimes it helps to cut up your draft and tape different parts together!)

If ...	After acknowledging what the child is doing well, you might say ...	Leave the writer with ...
The writer has some sections that have more writing and information than others. This writer seems to begin with a head of steam and then to peter out so that by the middle of a book, pages often hold only a single sentence.	You seem to always start your books by writing these lovely full pages that teach so much, but then after a bit, your pages get to be like this, and this. One thing that can help is to set a goal for how much you will write on a page. Make an X at the bottom of the page. See if you can write to that X. When you get there, set a new goal! This will help you get more and more ideas down on the page!	• Step 1: Set a goal. Make a star or an X on the page. • Step 2: Write to the goal as fast as you can. • Step 3: Set a new goal. ① Set a goal. ② ✗⊙ Write as fast as you can. ③ Set a new goal!

The Process of Revision

If ...	After acknowledging what the child is doing well, you might say ...	Leave the writer with ...
The writer is "done" before revising. This writer is perfectly pleased with his first draft and declares, "I'm done" soon after completing it. Your revision minilessons do little to help inspire this writer to revise, and you feel you must constantly sit by his side and point out parts to revise for him to do the work.	I've noticed that you often have trouble thinking of ways to revise your piece. You write a draft and then it feels done. Sometimes when it is hard to come up with ideas for improving your writing, it helps to have a published writer help. You just look at a published book that you love and notice cool things that the author has done, then you revise to do those same things in your writing.	When writers feel done, they study a few mentor texts asking, "What has this writer done that I could try as well?"
The writer does not have a large repertoire of strategies to draw from. This writer lives off of each day's minilesson. She is task-oriented and generally applies (or attempts to apply) what you teach each day. This student is living on your day-to-day teaching as if it is all she has, rather than drawing on a large repertoire of known writing techniques and strategies.	Whenever I teach something, I love to see kids like you go off and give it a go. It means they are pushing themselves to try new things. But I also hope that isn't *all* kids do. We've talked about how writers carry invisible backpacks full of strategies. When I teach a minilesson, I give you something new to add to your backpack, but it is important to use everything else you have in there too! Today, I want to teach you one way writers remind themselves of what they already know about revision. They look at artifacts like classroom charts and our Information Writing Checklist and look back at old entries to remind themselves of the strategies they know. Then, they write an action plan.	Take Action! 1. Look at charts, your notebook, and the Information Writing Checklist. 2. Make a list of the ways you could revise. 3. Create an action plan for yourself.
The writer is unsure how to revise her writing and does not use the tools available in the classroom. When this writer gets to the last page in her book, she may stop and get another booklet to begin a new text. The writer does not go back and try to add to her piece. She may or may not be aware of the charts, checklists, and mentor texts that she could use to help her decide how to revise her text.	Information writers revise as well. They use the same types of tools as other writers to help them revise their piece. Sometimes, studying a mentor text can help you find and think about what you may want to add or change in your own writing. One thing that I want to teach you is that you can study books and think, "What did this author do that was powerful in his writing? Can I do the same thing with my topic?"	A mentor text to help remind her to study books to find ideas for her writing. On a Post-it, write, "What did this author do that I can do?" What did this author do that I can do?

If ...	After acknowledging what the child is doing well, you might say ...	Leave the writer with ...
The writer tends to revise by elaborating, rather than narrowing and finding the focus of the text or chapter. When this writer revises, he may always revise to add information to his piece. Rarely will he think to take out something that doesn't go or to improve the way he has said something.	You are really good at adding things as you revise. Sometimes you add details, and sometimes you add things that will help make it so your writing makes sense. That's great. Congratulations. Now—can I teach you the next step? The next step as a reviser is to reread your writing, knowing that sometimes what the writing needs is for you to add, and sometimes the writing needs you to subtract! Like, if the book is called My Hamster and you get to a part that goes on and on about your turtle ... what would you need to do? You are right! Subtract. And what if you say "My hamster has a tiny tail" at the start of your book and then at the very end you say, "My hamster has a tiny tail." What if you repeated yourself by mistake? You are right! You'd subtract. Writers even do one more thing when they revise, they sometimes try to write the same thing with better words, or more excitement—revising not to add or subtract but to improve. If you ever do that, would you call me over?	Writers revise by: + adding (details, answers to readers questions) − subtracting (parts that don't belong, repetition ...) * improving (making the words better, making writing interesting)

The Process of Editing

The student has edited but has missed several mistakes or would otherwise benefit from learning to partner-edit. This writer often thinks she has written what she intended to say, and therefore she overlooks many mistakes. She would benefit from learning to edit with a partner before publishing her writing.	I know that you have worked hard to use many of the editing strategies you know and have made many changes to your piece. As a result, it is clearer and more readable. Sometimes as a writer, though, you know so clearly what you *wanted* to say that you miss places where you may have said something in a confusing or incorrect way. That's why most writers have editors that look at their writing once it's done. Today, I want to teach you a few things you and your writing partner can do together. You can: • Read your piece aloud and ask your partner to check to make sure what you say matches what he or she sees. • Circle words you think are misspelled and try to figure them out together. • Use the class editing checklist together.	A Few Things You and Your Writing Partner Might Say to Each Other • "Reread your piece, and I'll make sure what you say matches what I see." • "Let's circle the words that we think are misspelled and try them again." • "Let's use our class editing checklist to proofread your piece."

If …	After acknowledging what the child is doing well, you might say …	Leave the writer with …
The writer edits quickly and feels done, missing many errors. This writer tends to miss many errors because he does not reread his writing.	When you reread and edit your writing, it should take a little bit of time. You shouldn't feel like it was super fast. Editors are detectives, looking for mistakes that are hiding! One way to edit really carefully, like a detective, is to reread your writing *many* times, out loud, and slowly. Place your pen right under the words as you are reading. You might even reread a page a couple of times, just to be sure that no mistakes are hiding. Use the checklist in our room to help remind you of what kinds of things to be looking for as you are rereading.	Reread and Edit: • Spelling • Punctuation • Capitals Reread and Edit Spelling! the dog rn Capitals! Puncuation! ✓ The dog ran.
The writer has used an abundance of end punctuation marks throughout the text that do not make sense. This writer has end punctuation, such as periods, in strange and unusual places throughout the piece. For example, the writer might have end punctuation written down the page at the end of each line, regardless of whether that is the end of the sentence.	Writers reread and think carefully about where to place end punctuation. They think, "Does that sound right? Can I understand what I am teaching?" Sometimes reading it to a partner can help uncover the errors. After you find a mistake, you can change it. When you change it, though, check it the same way, "Does it sound right? Do I understand what I am teaching?"	Check End Punctuation: • Does that sound right? • Can I understand what I am teaching?

Opinion Writing

If ...	After acknowledging what the child is doing well, you might say ...	Leave the writer with ...
Structure and Cohesion		
The writer is new to the writing workshop or this particular genre of writing. This writer may be writing a story or an information text and may not understand how or why to write opinions.	You are writing a story—it tells what happened to you first, next, next. You want to be the kind of writer who can write different kinds of things. Like if you were a jewelry shop, you'd be glad if you could make pretty pins, but you'd also want to know how to make other things, too. And you wouldn't want to start off making a necklace and it looks like a little dog with a pin on the back! Well, today, you sort of did that. You started out making not a necklace but some opinion writing to change the world and you ended up making … a story again. When you write opinion pieces, instead of telling a story, you tell people how you feel about things in the world—things you really like or things you want to change. Then you say, "This is what I think, and this is why."	Story: I did this, and then this (or She did this, then this). Opinion writing: I think this. Here's why! You should think this way too. Story | Opinion I did this, then this, then this. | I think this because...
The writer dives into his piece without discussing the topic or introducing what the piece is about. This writer tends to give his opinion and may give supports, examples, and/or reasons, in any order. There does not seem to be a clear beginning, an order to the information, or a closing.	Writers plan their books. They think about how they are going to organize their information. Writers think about each part, from the beginning to the end. One way that you can work on the introduction of your book is to tell your readers about your topic, your opinion, and why they should read your book!	Things to Include in an Introduction: • Your topic • Your opinion • Why? Introduction Topic Opinion : why?

If ...	After acknowledging what the child is doing well, you might say ...	Leave the writer with ...
The writer's piece has ideas and information scattered throughout in a disorganized fashion. This writer has many disconnected parts to her writing. She may have information and opinions throughout the piece, but it lacks organization as well as consistent transitions that will bring more organization and structure to the piece and help the reader follow what the writer is teaching.	Writers try to organize their information in their books. Writers talk about each part of their idea as much as they can before they go on to another part of their piece. One way that you can organize your information and connect the different parts of your piece is to tell all about one piece of information. Then you can think to yourself, "Do I have another example?" Or you can say to yourself, "Also, another reason might be ..." This will help you not only connect your ideas, but it will also help you say more.	• "One example is ..." • "Another reason ..."
Elaboration		
The writer is struggling to elaborate. This writer has an opinion, as well as a reason or two to support that opinion, but most reasons are stated without elaboration. She may have created a long list of reasons to support her opinion but does not say more about any one reason or provide examples or evidence to support her reasons.	You know that when you give an opinion, you need to support it with reasons! But opinion writers don't just stop with reasons. Today, I want to teach you that when writers come up with reasons to support an opinion, they then try to find evidence. One way to do this is by writing, "For example ..." and then giving an example to support the reason.	Opinion + Reason + Evidence! To give evidence, try using, "for example ..." and then providing information that supports your idea.
The writer uses some elaboration strategies some of the time. This writer may elaborate on one page in his writing. But the writer does not continue to elaborate and use what he knows in other parts of his book.	One thing that you can do as a writer is to study your own best writing—and then try to do that best writing on every page. I say this because on this page, you used a very fancy technique to elaborate ... let me show you ... So what do you think you should be doing on this page? And this one?	Study great writers: like YOU!!! What did I do on one page (in one part) that I can do on every page (in every part?) Page 1: Page 2: Page 3: I compared two things!!!! Page 4:
The writer's piece lacks voice. This writer's piece sounds very formulaic. She doesn't yet really talk to the reader.	Right now, will you tell me a bit about this? What do you think? Oh ... and can you explain why you think that? You know what—one of the most important things that writers learn is that great writing sounds a lot like the writer is talking to the reader. Let me say back what you just said to me because these words are full of what people call voice. These are the words you should put onto the page when you write. Listen ... I'm telling you this because the way you wrote this book, and this one too, and this one, it feels like a machine could have written that. It doesn't *sound* like you. Would you work on making your writing sound more like you? The best way to do that is to do what you just did—say aloud what you want to write, and say it like you are talking to another person. Then put those words onto the paper.	At the top of each page, draw a face with a speech balloon coming out of the mouth to remind the writer to first say it to someone, trying to talk like she really cares about it. Remind the writer that you'll check to see if it actually sounds like the writer (not a machine) wrote it when you read her writing.

If ...	After acknowledging what the child is doing well, you might say ...	Leave the writer with ...
The writer has provided evidence, usually in a one line summary statement. It would be a step forward for this writer to sometimes write her evidence as a Small Moment story, or as a list.	I love that you are giving evidence to support your reasons. Like when you said, "Animal Planet is a great show because it teaches you things" and then you said, "I learned a lot about climbing a mountain in Alaska," that is great. You are giving evidence to support the fact that you learn from the show. But you know what? It would be even better if you wrote in a way so that we can almost feel like we were watching the show, and we were learning from it, too. You might say, "For example, in the how ..." and then tell a story about one thing that happened in the show and tell what you learned from it. That way we could really feel like your evidence is our evidence too.	When writing an opinion piece, you can support your ideas with: Stories, and tell what you learned from them Examples (write them with details.)
Language		
The writer struggles with spelling. This writer's piece is riddled with spelling mistakes. This does not necessarily mean the writing is not strong (in fact, the essay he wrote may be very strong), but the spelling mistakes compromise the reader's ability to understand it. The writer's struggle with spelling may stem from various causes—difficulty with understanding and applying spelling patterns, a limited stock of high-frequency words, lack of investment, the acquisition of English as a new language—and diagnosing the underlying problem will be an important precursor to teaching into it.	When an opinion piece (or any piece of writing, really) is full of spelling mistakes, it can be hard for readers to understand what you are trying to say. Today, I want to remind you that writers try out multiple ways to spell a word before settling on one. Then, if they are still stuck, they consult a friend, writing partner, word wall, or other classroom resource.	Writers work hard at their spelling. They: 1. Try multiple versions of a word in the margin 2. Pick the one that looks right 3. Consult a peer, word wall, or other resource to help

If ...	After acknowledging what the child is doing well, you might say ...	Leave the writer with ...
The writer struggles to write longer or "harder" words on the page. When the writer encounters something new or something that he needs to approximate, he freezes up. This writer might not feel comfortable writing words he doesn't already know. For instance, the writer may be stymied by writing the word *delicious*. The writer may stop writing or may write the word *good* instead.	Sometimes it seems to me that you are about to write really long and hard words, and then you start thinking, "Oh no, maybe I won't spell them right. Oh no, maybe I'll make a mistake, Oh no, Oh no." (I've meanwhile been shaking in my boots.) When you feel like you might chicken out because you are worried about making a mistake—say to yourself, "Stop it! Be Brave!" And then, even though you aren't sure, just try the best you can and keep going. That's the way to get the best writing onto the page. If you chicken out from writing big words, or from writing the little details that can help a reader, or from trying to say something in a really beautiful way, your writing ends up just being so-so. The only way to make great writing is to be a brave writer. And to be a brave writer of long and hard words, you can think about each part of the word and think if you know other words that sound the same as that one. You can even try the same word a couple of times. Then you can pick the one that sounds the best and looks right.	Be BRAVE! Think about the parts of the word as you spell. pumpkin pump/kin
The writer struggles with comma usage. This writer is attempting to form more complex sentences but is struggling with the process. It may be that she uses commas incorrectly, interspersing them throughout the piece with no apparent rhyme or reason, or that she simply doesn't use commas, resulting in long, difficult-to-read sentences. Either way, this writer needs help understanding how commas are used in sentences.	I've noticed that you've been trying to write longer, more complex sentences. Because of this, your writing sounds more like talking. It is quite beautiful. When writers write sentences that are more complex, though, they often need to use commas. Commas help readers know where to pause and help the sentence make sense. Today, I want to teach you a few important ways that writers use commas. Writers use commas in lists, and they also use them to separate two or more descriptive words.	Use commas ... To separate items in a list: • I want pears, apples, and oranges. To separate descriptive words: • He drove by in his red, shiny car.
The writer tends not to use specific and precise language as he writes about his opinions. This writer writes with generalizations. ("We need stuff because it is good. It is nice. It is great.")	I want to tell you something about your writing. You tend to write with big general words, and it is usually better to write with exact words. Like instead of saying, "Our coat closet is bad," it would be better to say it with exact words. "Our coat closet is ..." What? Messy? A snarl of coats? It looks like people just throw things anywhere? You see how it is better to use exact words than big general words like, "It is bad." Try asking yourself, "What *exactly* do I want to say?" Think about one way to say it, then think about another way.	What EXACTLY do I want to say? Think about one way ... then think about another way!

The Process of Generating Ideas

The writer struggles to generate meaningful topics worth exploring. This writer feels stuck and has difficulty generating ideas for writing. Sometimes this manifests through avoidance behaviors (going to the bathroom, sharpening pencils), and other times the child simply seems to be in a constant state of "thinking," not writing. This child needs help not only with generating ideas, but also with learning to independently use a repertoire of strategies when stuck.	I've noticed that coming up with ideas has been hard for you and that you've had to spend a lot of time thinking about what to write. When you write opinion pieces, you want them to be persuasive. And for them to be persuasive, you have to *care* a lot about the topic! It can help to think about what you really care the most about—think about things you love or hate … and then see if you can write opinion pieces about that.	Write what you love, write what you hate. Not in between.

The Process of Drafting

The writer doesn't have a plan before he begins to write. This writer seems to pick up his or her pen, and write what he or she wants, and then is stymied. The writer might then start an ending to the piece, only to decide more needs to be said. This can lead to a piece that is chaotic, or that has a sequence of four endings.	One thing I notice about you is that when you write, you sit down at your desk, pick up your pen, and you get started. Lots of kids wait and wait and wait to think up an idea, but you don't wait. Ideas come to you right away, and that is great. But I want to teach you that when an idea comes to you, it is good to *not* get started writing but to instead spend some time getting ready. The way writers get ready is they plan what they are going to say so that before they write a word, they have a whole lot of ideas for what will go at the beginning of the piece, and in the middle … I think it would help you plan your opinion pieces if you did some drawings before you start writing—planning drawings. Maybe you could try starting with a drawing of the problem, then one or two drawings of what you think people could do, step one and step two, to fix the problem, and then a drawing of what things will be like when they are fixed up. So today you are writing about the park being messy—what will go in the first drawing, the drawing about the problem? Ok—so beautiful birds and flowers and then garbage. Will you put some details in—like show a daffodil with a paper cup smushed right on it? Great! Then that drawing will help you plan out about six things you can say about the problem!	A Post-it that helps remind him how to get words down on the page. You may write, "Use your plan." There may be an icon of a page of writing with picture space and writing space. There should be an arrow pointing to the picture space for the writer to use to help add to his words.  Planning paper—two pages taped together, divided into four columns that are labeled: Problem Fixing it, step 1 Fixing it, step 2 The solution

If ...	After acknowledging what the child is doing well, you might say ...	Leave the writer with ...
The Process of Revision		
The writer fills the pages as she drafts and only writes to the bottom of the page when she revises. This writer tends to push herself while she drafts to write to the end of the page. The writer, therefore, sometimes feels like she cannot or does not need to revise because there is not enough space.	It seems like you get to the end of the page, when you are writing, and you stop there. But lots of times, I am pretty sure you have more to say—but you aren't going to page two, or adding on a flap at the ending. After this, will you remember that writers write as much as they have to say ... and they make their books longer, their pages longer, so they can say everything? They ask themselves, "Do I have more to say?" And if have more to say, they *find* the space. They *make* the space. Whenever you want to add more, you can think, "Should I add a flap or a whole new page?" And then just tape or staple it in!	Extra flaps and strips to use and add onto her page. To help the writer to remember to use these tools again the next day, you may tuck a few into her writing folder. This way, as she is trying to add more, she will have a few flaps ready to add on. You may leave a Post-it that reminds her to add on to her writing. It may say, "Revise" at the top, and underneath it may say, "Add on information, examples, and reasons."
The writer tends to have a limited repertoire of elaboration strategies. This writer elaborates by adding on to his piece with the same strategy, rather than using a few ways to say and add more.	I notice that you elaborate by (strategy the writer is using) in your opinion books, and that is great. BUT writers try to write with a variety of stuff. So I wanted to remind you that opinion writers also say more by adding in these things: Tips on how to do something Suggestions on the best ways to do something Warnings about what could go wrong Stories of other people who have done this Encouragement to do this Let's reread your piece and think about which ones we can add.	If you made a whole-class chart on ways to elaborate in opinion writing, you could make a mini-version of that chart for the child's writing folder, or you could turn that chart into a checklist.
The writer tends to give information and reasons that are not connected to her original opinion. This writer often starts with an opinion and in the middle of the piece may find herself writing about something else or giving information that doesn't help the reader understand or believe in her opinion.	Writers reread their writing and revise their pieces to make sure that the details and information they are giving fit with their opinions. One way you can check for this is you can reread your piece and ask yourself, "Do the information and reasons go with my opinion?" If they don't, you can cross them out.	A chart that on one side says, "Fits with my information." and on the other side says, "Does not fit with my information."

If ...	After acknowledging what the child is doing well, you might say ...	Leave the writer with ...
The Process of Editing		
The writer edits for one thing but not for others. This writer may edit her work but only tries to fix her spelling. She may not reread to fix her punctuation.	When writers edit, there are many things that they look for and try to fix. You can use a checklist to help you think about editing for many things. You may want to reread your piece a few times, looking for different things each time.	Reread and Edit! • Spelling • Punctuation • Capitals
The writer only uses or knows one way to edit her spelling. This writer may feel like she has edited her spelling, even if few words are actually fixed. This may be because she does not have or use a repertoire of ways to work on spelling. For example, she may only check her piece for word wall words. She may not try out multisyllabic words in different ways to help get a closer approximation or the correct spelling.	Young writers use more than one strategy to spell. As you are spelling a word, you can try to think about what is the best way to spell this word—the word wall, trying to write and rewrite the word a few times, or looking it up in a resource in the room.	Try Different Spellings: 1. _____ 2. _____ 3. _____